RACE TO WIN

RACE TO WIN

How to Become a Complete Champion Driver

Derek Daly

MOTORBOOKS

First published in 2008 by Motorbooks, an imprint of MBI Publishing Company LLC, Galtier Plaza, Suite 200, 380 Jackson Street, St. Paul, MN 55101 USA

Motorbooks titles are also available at discounts in bulk quantity for industrial or sales-promotional use. For details write to Special Sales Manager at MBI Publishing Company, Galtier Plaza, Suite 200, 380 Jackson Street, St. Paul, MN 55101 USA.

To find out more about our books, join us online at www.motorbooks.com.

ISBN-13: 978-0-7603-3185-9

Editors: Lindsay Hitch and Lee Klancher
Interior Design: Jennifer Maass
Cover Design: Tom Heffron

Printed in the United States of America

Library of Congress Cataloging-in-Publication Data

Daly, Derek, 1953–
  Race to win: how to become a complete champion driver/by Derek Daly; foreword by Mario Andretti.
    p. cm.
  ISBN 978-0-7603-3185-9 (softboundhardbound w/jacket)
  1. Automobile racing—Vocational guidance. 2. Automobile racing drivers. I. Andretti, Mario, 1940– II. Title.
GV1029.D246 2008
796.72—dc22
                            2007030876

On the cover: Nick Heidfeld, fifth position, leads Fernando Alonso, seventh position, and Nico Rosberg, ninth position, in the 2007 French Grand Prix. Kimi Räikkönen won the race for the Ferrari team. *LAT*

On the back cover: Derek Daly and Mario Andretti share a light-hearted moment. *Derek Daly collection*

CONTENTS

FOREWORD

I'm often asked what it takes to become successful in motor racing. I never know quite what to say, mostly because there is no short answer. I know what it took for *me* to be successful, but I certainly can't explain it in five minutes—maybe not even five hours. It's just too complex.

So when Derek Daly told me he had written a book on how to become successful in motor racing, I was intrigued. The more I read, the more impressed I became with his effort. The book offers a true driver-development path laid out for drivers, team managers, and parents to follow.

I was particularly impressed with his Champion's Pyramid, which has six qualities that a driver needs to possess (and balance) to succeed. The more balance, the more success. Every element is there—and they're all important. Like baking a cake, no single ingredient is the most important. Miss one, and the whole cake is ruined.

But I think the most fascinating aspect of the book is the number of anecdotes that Derek uses. He cites real drivers and countless scenarios to make his points—and he didn't make this stuff up. It's an examination and breakdown of drivers that results in valuable insight and coaching. My hope is that in reading this someone quickly learns a lesson it took guys like me years to learn. Quite honestly, the lessons in this book could resonate far beyond the racing industry.

I believe it takes a focused, systematic approach to become successful in racing today. And Derek's years of racing at the highest levels, along with his time observing drivers from the broadcast booth, have given him the frame of reference and expertise needed to clearly articulate the required ingredients to succeed as a race driver. The result is a book that is extremely worthwhile and straightforward. For sure, the next time someone asks me what it takes to become a driving champion, I'll have an answer: "Read Derek's book."

—Mario Andretti

THE PURSUIT OF EXCELLENCE

This is a book about a subject that is very close to my heart: the development of a champion race car driver. I have spent most of my adult life immersed in the colorful, glamorous, and exciting world of Formula One, Indy cars, and World Sports cars, and all this despite my humble beginnings as the son of a middle-class grocery store owner in Dublin, Ireland.

I won many championships along the way in the lower formulae, however, I never became a champion at the highest levels (ranked 10th in the Formula One World Championship in 1980), nor did I win an Indy car race (third place in

Milwaukee being the best) or a Grand Prix (although I came very close in Monaco in 1982, when I led on the second-to-last lap only to have the gearbox fail).

While I competed across the globe in Formula One from 1978 to 1982, I began to struggle to maintain the form that had been so natural for me in the lower formulae. I began to wonder why, and that led me to years of fascinating studies about why some drivers grow to become successful champions and what the difference really is between good and great. Many will tell you that to be successful in anything you have to have killer instincts. Well, this book will show you that becoming a legendary motorsports champion requires a whole lot more.

I've personally made all (or most of) the classic mistakes. I derailed my career many times and had to come back from self-destruction several times. I experienced what I grew to know as "the genesis of self-sabotage." That experience, along with a career as a broadcaster spent watching the best of the best on the track week in and week out, gives me a unique perspective on what it takes to succeed in this demanding career.

I hope that the hard lessons I've learned can direct a few young drivers down the path to success. I will also use real-life examples of some of the established great drivers to clearly show that there is no magic bullet when you shoot for success. There is, however, a clear list of ingredients necessary to become a champion.

As you read this book, I hope you will see yourself in the examples. I want you to see yourself and the path you might have taken, might be taking, or might be able to take in the future. As you read the different chapters, please remember that your ultimate success will be a product of your choices. Please also remember that some of the information in this book is somewhat age-sensitive, so don't expect your eight-year-old karter to understand all that is contained herein.

I have spent many years studying the great champions. I have asked many probing questions. I have consulted with many professional journalists, and I now know that there are six key elements necessary for building what I call the Champion's Pyramid. They are talent identification, technical ability, communication skills, mental skills, physical skills, and, lastly, desire and commitment.

In this book, I'll explain each of the concepts and how they relate to driving and give examples of great drivers who display good and bad traits in each category. I'll also offer practical advice showing you how to get the best out of yourself in each category.

Analogies are used throughout this book. Most people are visual learners, and I want to "paint the picture" as much as possible. For that reason, I've also developed a visual version of the Champion's Pyramid.

If you follow my guidance, I believe you can improve as a driver to the point that you reach your personal limits. For some, that may mean finishing fifth in their class racing karts. For a very special few, that means standing on the top of the podium at the highest levels of our sport.

For everyone who reads this book, I want it to mean that you become the very best you can personally be.

— Derek Daly
April 9, 2007

CHAPTER 1

THE CHAMPION'S PYRAMID

The best drivers are the ones who take control of their environment, develop all six ingredients necessary to success, and understand the principles of working in a team.

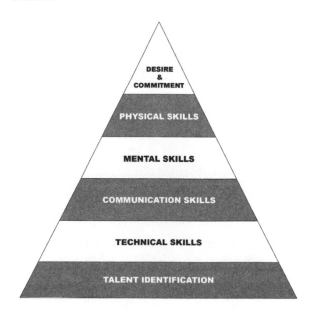

The Champion's Pyramid, which has equal-length sides, represents the balance of qualities that a champion driver needs to possess in order to succeed. The enclosed illustration is a simple pictorial description of what a champion is aiming to build. This book will explain, step by step, why each element is necessary and how to develop those elements.

As you study the Champion's Pyramid, keep in mind that all through your racing career, you are aiming for a balanced triangle. Every race and test session will alter the triangle because the knowledge and/or experience changes with every lap that you do in a race car. In order to consistently perform at a high level, the pyramid needs to be balanced, and each element needs to be well developed.

For example, if you have a wealth of technical knowledge but are short on communication and mental skills, your personal pyramid will be unbalanced. The more balanced the package the more successful you will be and the longer the success will last.

RESEARCH

In 1996, Bob Earl—my former Nissan GTP teammate—and I created one of the most comprehensive driver-development programs in America. It was called the Team Green Academy and was created on behalf of Brown & Williamson (under the Kool cigarette brand), then a major CART Champ Car sponsor. Bob was a very good driver and an even better teacher-coach.

Bob was exceptionally good at creating driving exercises and environments that really stretched drivers. That program gave me direct access to the physical, emotional, and mental make-up of 46 young potential stars of American motorsports. It was an eye-opener and a fascinating look into what made some drivers tick . . . and what derailed them.

What I hear most of all from young drivers are the reasons why they can't do something. No one will pay for their privilege to race cars, so they stop. If that's the case, they should stop, because they were never going to make it anyway. No matter how much driving talent you have, if you do not possess the desire and commitment to keep going when times get tough, you will fail. There is no real magic to becoming a champion, but you do have to have all the ingredients necessary to be successful.

The best drivers are the ones who take control of their environment, develop all six ingredients necessary to succeed, and understand the principles of working in a team environment. You'll come to understand that the most complete drivers in the world were not necessarily born that way; they were developed and trained to be champions.

I have drawn upon the professional knowledge of many of the world's most respected journalists. They are professionals (and mostly friends of mine) who scrutinize every aspect of the world's greatest race car drivers. Their insights have proven invaluable as I have gathered the type of illustrative information needed to present the content in this book in the most emotionally engaging way.

EVERY RACE CAR DRIVER IS A LITTLE DIFFERENT

Drivers come in many shapes and sizes, and many have been very successful in different eras. It's almost impossible to compare drivers from different eras because of the different equipment and knowledge that was available to them.

Teammates are always compared because they are largely in equal equipment. There is no doubt that motorsports has a way of physically and mentally challenging drivers (and team members).

Three-time Champ Car champion, Frenchman Sébastien Bourdais, was refreshingly different when quizzed on the blatant disparity in relative performance between Brazilian Bruno Junqueira (his teammate) and himself, between 2003 and 2004.

"This year we made some changes—one was a big one that helps the balance, but I'm not going to say what it was.

GENDER LANGUAGE

Note that this book uses the male pronoun throughout. We've done that not to take anything away from the contingent of great female drivers on the track in the past, present, and future, but simply for the economy of language.

It definitely made the car faster, but it doesn't suit Bruno's racing style as much as it does mine.

"The other difference is Bruno is making a lot of mistakes this year, because he is trying very hard. And when you make mistakes like he made in practice at Laguna, you screw yourself for the race."

So we can only take from this that the mental skills are a little different between these teammates. You will also understand as you read Chapter Five that a driver often makes comments designed to destabilize another driver mentally, especially if he can't beat him with outright speed.

STANDOUT CHAMPIONS

From all the drivers I have seen in the modern era, four stand out as being very special: Formula One world champion, Indy car champion, and Indy 500/Daytona 500 winner Mario Andretti; three-time Formula One world champion Ayrton Senna from Brazil; four-time Formula One world champion Alain Prost from France; and seven-time Formula One world champion Michael Schumacher from Germany. I make no apologies for choosing Formula One drivers because I believe that Formula One is the most competitive, intense, and challenging motorsport on the planet.

These drivers were very different but all became a part of history because of the way they applied themselves to the task of motor racing. Senna was emotionally driven, Schumacher was mentally driven, Prost was mission driven, and Andretti was commitment driven.

These are four very different drivers both physically and mentally, and you could debate which of them is the best race driver. There is no doubt, however, that if you want to emulate a great motorsports champion, you could not pick four better models than Andretti, Prost, Schumacher, and Senna. Throughout this book, these four (particularly Schumacher) will be contrasted with drivers of today and yesterday in order to uncover what makes the difference between a very good driver and a great champion.

British journalist Mark Hughes offered this insightful comparison of Senna, Prost, and Schumacher:

"The impression is that the Ferrari [Schumacher's] cockpit is a rather colder, quieter place than was Senna's.

"However, to believe that all this order, rationality, and cerebral control is more formidable than the hormonal rush of Senna at work is to discount the unbelievable territory to which those emotions—and probably his religious convictions too—gained Senna access. He could channel his feelings to pull out a qualifying lap like that at Monaco '88, where from within the deep reaches of his soul he found two point five seconds. Such things should not have been possible. At the same place the next year, he was playing nip and tuck with Prost for pole when, out of the blue, he produced a lap one point one second quicker than anything his rival could manage. Some even wondered if the timing machinery had malfunctioned.

"That is what Senna at his best could do—make you doubt your senses.

"Schumacher has many times produced performances that have reduced his opponents to bit players, but it has invariably been—like Barcelona '96—in compromised conditions. That day he was lapping sometimes six seconds faster than anyone else in the rain, and doing it with a lightness of touch that made it seem like child's play.

"Alain Prost was known as 'The Professor.' He was meticulous in his preparation, and his execution during a race was flawless. His prerace planning was second to none, and his emotional and mental control was admired at all times. Both Senna and Schumacher were known for emotional (and irrational) outbursts in the car. Prost never did such a thing. Senna was flamboyant, Schumacher was a machine, and Prost was a calculator."

Mario was a combination of everything necessary to be a champion. He covered many eras and, perhaps in addition to his skills, he exhibited as strong a desire and commitment to the sport as has ever been seen.

However, the greatest example of a driver developing the complete package necessary to become a champion would be Michael Schumacher. He is the greatest driver of the modern era. He could well be the greatest driver of all time. Michael went through several critical stages of his career, but he never lost sight of what his job ultimately was and what it would take to be the very best he could be. Michael had a fully developed Champion's Pyramid.

Perhaps the finest example of Schumacher's well-rounded driving ability was when he made the nearly unprecedented move from Benetton to Ferrari for the 1996 season. He was a world champion with the Benetton team, and Ferrari at that time was not a good team. During his early and sometimes trying times, Schumacher drew upon his multiple on- and off-track skills to build the type of environment he needed to win. He never criticized Ferrari, even when the car did not match his obvious skills. He always helped and supported the team and always wore a smile even if he was not on the podium. His classy behavior built an almost unshakable foundation of critical trust and belief within the team.

Celebrated Irish journalist, and a good friend of mine, Maurice Hamilton also recognized Michael Schumacher's off-track abilities. Hamilton wrote in the American magazine *Racer* at the end of the 2002 season:

"Since coming to the Modena in '96, he has been the catalyst most responsible for pulling racing's most celebrated team up from mediocrity to a period of unrivaled dominance. It was Schumacher, after all, who helped assemble the Ferrari brain trust of Jean Todt, Ross Brawn, and Rory Byrne; and it's Schumacher who is adored and respected by the hundreds of anonymous engineers, technicians and mechanics who make the Scuderia fire on all ten cylinders.

"A very big plus in his favor is the way he has worked very hard at molding that team around him," noted Maurice. "He took the hard route by choosing to go to Ferrari instead of Williams; has worked the team around him like nobody else has done; and has got this ability to work, work, work and have the total affection and the dedication of the team. That's always the sign of a good champion."

When former Arrows Formula One team owner Tom Walkinshaw ran the Benetton Formula One team, he said, "Michael Schumacher's greatness as a driver is displayed by the fact that he can win in a car that is not the fastest in the field."

Michael Schumacher has it all, and this book will give you some of the reasons why. Even four-time Formula One world champion Alain Prost saw Schumacher as a special talent who understood how to create the right environment in which to flourish.

In a French magazine interview, Prost related how he admired the part Schumacher played in turning Ferrari around, as well as his ability to make a team revolve around him, much as Senna did.

"Obviously, Michael took on a great challenge when he went there. The biggest challenge is to bring an unsuccessful team to the top, and okay, Ferrari was not a small team, but it was not winning much. It was a difficult move from Benetton, where he was world champion, to Ferrari. He never criticized them even when the team and the car were not good; he always helped the team and he was always smiling when he was third or fourth. And I really like that about him. I think he has created a good ambience there and that's what I admire about him the most."

In 2002, British journalist Jonathan Noble talked with Schumacher and got a glimpse of why he is so great.

"My philosophy is never to think you have achieved it," Schumacher said. "You always have to look at what you can do different and what you can do better with the car and with yourself. And you will always find little things. You have to do things differently because the moment will require it. You have to be flexible enough to see it and be open to see it."

Noble believes one of Schumacher's racing strengths was that he consistently found ways to boost his own motivation.

"But then the good thing is that you will do three days of going around and around and around with nothing happening, because you are working on the same area, and suddenly on the last day you find two tenths," Schumacher explains. "Up goes your motivation again. You are always looking for it and you always feel that when something reasonable happens, it was worth it."

Noble also notes that Schumacher shone brightest in race conditions because of his innate ability in good, average, and even bad cars. Ferrari sporting director Jean Todt said, "We know very well that Michael's biggest strength is to be able to get the best out of even a very difficult car to drive."

One of my favorite journalists is England's Mark Hughes. Hughes has studied Schumacher from every angle. In a feature printed in England's premier motorsports magazine, *Autosport*, Hughes had these fascinating insights into someone I consider to be the most complete race car driver ever:

"Neither his driving style—early turn in, not much steering lock, using the brakes to aid direction change—nor his racing style—flat-out attack start-to-finish, utilizing his supreme fitness to make every single lap count—have changed much over the years.

"It is the latter point that is remarkable. After more than a decade at the top of the sport, a driver will usually be relying less on raw speed, more on experience. That's how it was for Niki Lauda, say, or Alain Prost. But such an approach wouldn't be appropriate to today's [2002] fuel stop format of Formula One, where races comprise two or three stints of flat-out running and where looking after tyres, gearboxes and engines isn't such an issue. Try to back off from the raw edge in this era, and you'd soon be discovered. There's no hint of it from Schuey."

Hughes added that fitness and Schumacher's ability to control his emotions have also been crucial to his success. He credits the fact that Schumacher built a team around him that supported him, and he supported them in return, as something that kept him level and focused, and that team has been key to his longevity.

Hughes continued: "There is no doubt he (Schumacher) is joyous and charming if he wins, and he denies that his ruthlessness to defend his position in a race—most notably his fabled 'chops' on rivals—is anything out of the ordinary.

"There is undoubtedly a degree of humbleness about Michael Schumacher. He clearly knows he is the best man out there at the moment, but steadfastly refuses to rub such a fact in to his rivals."

"I pay as much respect to everyone—because we all eat, drink and come from the same base," Schumacher said.

Former Schumacher teammate at Ferrari, Eddie Irvine, said that, "The easy bit is to be as quick as Michael in a good car. Far harder is to be anywhere near him in a bad one."

It does not necessarily mean that upbringing or family environment have anything to do with whether a driver makes it to the top or not. All people (including siblings) are born with different temperaments, instincts, responses, and belief systems. Look at the Schumacher brothers, Michael and Ralf. They grew up in the same house, yet they are driven completely differently, with Ralf struggling to keep up with Michael's desire and commitment.

In October 2004, British journalist Adam Cooper compared the two with no punches pulled. He wrote:

"Sometimes Ralf Schumacher drives like his brother, sometimes like a granny."

Cooper's point refers to Ralf Schumacher's apparent inconsistency and, secondly, his off-track persona. The guy is not known for being media-friendly or, judging by the tales that have emerged from the Williams team over the years, much of a team player.

He denies that brother Michael's experience at Ferrari serves as an inspiration, but clearly there is a parallel. He wants to be the guy around whom the team is built, whose experience is acknowledged and respected.

No one would have questioned any team signing Ralf Schumacher in the middle of the 2003 season or Italian Jarno Trulli in the middle of the 2004 season, when both men were on highs. The curious thing is that both are noted for putting in stunning performances when they are happy with the set-up, but for struggling when things are not just so. Hitherto, all Formula One cars to have emerged from Toyota have been anything but consistent.

Cooper also points out that Ralf Schumacher's success will be tied to his ability to fully commit himself to PR and media activities in the future. You might think press relations irrelevant if the guy is quick, but in this media-dominated age, it does matter—a lot.

As does motivating the guys on the team, something that Mark Webber and Jenson Button do so well. Cooper also noted that when Ralf joined the Toyota Formula One team, he had the chance to become an inspiring leader, especially as he shared a language with much of the crew. Whether he's up to that role would be shown over the coming seasons.

THE RIGHT ENVIRONMENT

To extract the very best from any athlete (or child), you have to surround them with the type of environment that helps them flourish.

If you have ever questioned why the right environment is important for drivers, consider what Renault Executive Director of Engineering Pat Symonds said to Mark Hughes in November 2004 about British Formula One star Jenson Button. Button had a trying time at Renault and, despite his talents, rewards were not forthcoming.

Button's driving style is beautifully stylish and very quick. His steering inputs are minimal, and he appears to rely less on braking to aid the direction change. When he was struggling at Renault, the technical core of the team was unsympathetic to the problems he was having in fine-tuning the car to his natural style.

Symonds later said, "I don't think we saw what we had. Everything we've seen subsequently suggests we failed to extract his potential."

After Button's move to British American Racing (BAR), he found his true level and was able to do what he was unable to accomplish as a younger guy in a less sympathetic environment—dig deep. He's been able to work on areas of weakness: at Monza, for example, we saw a Button who, for the first time, was a ruthlessly effective overtaker.

Hughes continues: "It's too simplistic to say Button's form has just followed that of the cars he's been given to drive and that all we're seeing is a good driver in a good car. Driving racing cars at this level is an activity too delicately poised on the point of inner calm and confidence for that equation ever to hold up. Simplistic reasoning might say that Giancarlo Fisichella annihilated Button in the same car in 2001 and therefore could do so again, or that the BAR 006 was even better than Button made it look. That may be true, but it's doubtful.

"Just watching Button drive in '01 and comparing it to the year before, it was very obvious he wasn't achieving his potential, wasn't getting what he needed from the car."

At the Formula One world championship level (or any level), it's about finding your groove, locking onto it, and molding things around you to hold that groove. Only then do you have full access to your talent, and that's rarely achieved.

This book is designed to unlock your potential. There is no magic to being successful in racing, but you need to know how to find your groove; you need to know how to create the environment within which you will shine. You need to know what to develop and how to develop it, and when you develop all areas of the Champion's Pyramid, you will be a powerhouse. Most importantly, you will be the best you can be.

RACING DNA

Every person on this planet is born with strengths and weaknesses. I don't believe that a race car driver is ever born with all the strengths he needs to become a great champion. Every driver possesses a unique makeup. I call this makeup "racing DNA" (R-DNA). That R-DNA might be similar in some areas to other drivers, but the combination is unique to each driver. Within that R-DNA will be several characteristics that will be on display every time a driver performs. These characteristics are the driver's strengths and weaknesses, and they are the driver's passport to success or failure.

Unlike your human DNA, your R-DNA can be altered. For example, everyone is born with a certain body shape; however, each one of us can determine how our bodies look and act. We can overeat and become less active, or we can work at having a different and more active look and ability.

What you look like is a product of the decisions you make, just as how you race is a product of the decisions you make. Remember: choice equals change. Change can be threatening for many people, since oftentimes it requires an element of discomfort because it can expose your fears—fears of the unknown, fears of failure, or just fears of exposing your weaknesses.

How you perform as a driver is also a direct result of decisions you make. The level a driver achieves will be directly related to the development of all six areas of the Champion's Pyramid.

Throughout this book, I will break down each of these profiles and show you through example what separates the good from the great.

WHAT IS DRIVER DEVELOPMENT?

It really is amazing to me that, with so much at stake in professional motorsports, there has never really been a structured driver-development program at the highest specialized levels, in America or Europe. I have seen many that I would call "driver-assistance" programs that attempt to masquerade as development programs, but I've never seen the real thing.

Driver-assistance programs provide support, sometimes financial, sometimes just equipment. However, no matter what sponsorship or equipment you have, without all the skills necessary to get the best from it, it can be a wasted investment.

Why do you think other professional sports have team coaching and also specialized coaching for specific positions? How good would NFL quarterbacks Joe Montana or Dan Marino have become if they were subjected to generalized coaching instead of specialized coaching. How good would Tiger Woods be if he did not enjoy specialized coaching?

Motor racing should be the same. If you could develop the next Michael Schumacher or Mario Andretti or even the next best thing, it could pay back huge dividends. Ferrari could never afford to buy the type of positive exposure that Schumacher generated for them through his technical ability, his ability to energize the team, and of course his sheer driving ability. Was the $25 million (rumored) that Ferrari paid him expensive or a good value? I think it was a good value because it was less than 10 percent of Ferrari's overall race budget.

For many years, certainly in America, a variety of racing schools have promoted their driver-development programs. The reality is that most racing schools don't know what it takes to develop a champion driver, and they have never had a genuine driver-development program (at the highest levels). Their main concentration tends to be on-track coaching, which is very valuable but just one component of the complete package. Red Bull has what it calls a driver-development program, but it concentrates almost exclusively on physical preparedness and hoped-for, good on-track performance.

Since 1994, former Indy car driver Lyn St. James has provided a well-structured driver-development program (she has a good idea what's needed because she has lived it), but it has limitations because of the amount of money it takes to run a specialized program at the highest levels.

Drivers need to be developed individually. Not only do they need to be accurately evaluated and then coached individually, they need to be made aware of what will be necessary when the big time comes knocking. Simply supplying money and/or equipment is like sending a student with a desire to be a scientist to a neighborhood school. Sure, he will learn a lot, and he will progress, but he will never reach great heights without specialized schooling. Grids today are full of drivers who have been hugely successful relying on their instincts and reflexes. This book is designed to take you much deeper and give you a foundation that will not be easily rocked and a knowledge that can make you the best you can ever be. No one can ask for more than that.

The key to real driver development is how you position yourself to get the very best from yourself and therefore reap the rewards and the financial benefits. No driver could ever complain if, during his career, he was able to achieve his very best. To become the very best you can be in motorsports is not a black art. To develop a driver to be the best he can be is not a black art either. It is a clear path that must be understood and one that has always generated many questions. This book is designed to give you those answers, and it is designed to be a foundation for driver development unlike anything motorsports has seen before.

EARLY LEARNING DAYS IN FORMULA ONE

When I drove for the March Formula One team in 1981, March founder/designer (and my personal engineer) Robin Herd regularly made the statement that, "There is absolutely no magic to being successful in motorsports. You just need a competitive driver, competitive car, and enough money in the budget."

The budget is a critical part of the equation. It will also be an ever-changing number that needs to be big enough to provide and service the equipment and personnel, and managed well enough to last the full season. The commercial side of a team can be very fractured and complicated, and it really needs to be handled by trained professionals.

The car is an ever-changing technical package that needs to be constantly adjusted and developed to give the best compromise of chassis set-up for tracks and conditions. The team is expected to shoulder most of this load by working with accurate information from a driver and/or computer data to create a competitive race car.

There is an indefinite number of settings that make up the best compromise for race car handling, and usually the stronger the engineering department of the team, the more accurately they can find the right set-up.

In my opinion, the driver is by far the most complex part of the puzzle and by far the most important. The driver is an ever-changing and maturing package that needs to be constantly developed and managed. The driver is the human element that is born with an R-DNA that is manifested through his physical, mental, and spiritual attributes, but more importantly the driver is born with both strengths and weaknesses.

My hope is that you will be open and honest enough to see yourself in the examples in this book, and then you will set a path for yourself, armed with the knowledge of what it takes to become a champion.

RELATIONSHIPS

One of the first things you need to know and fully understand is that motor racing is very much a relationship business. The first impressions you create can be long-lasting. Your traits, strengths, and weaknesses will become apparent to all the people who matter. All the teams talk to each other; your driving talents will be the subject of discussion with any team owner/manager prior to hiring you.

A team owner that you meet at a very young age could well be your boss two or three decades later. The media will get to know and scrutinize your abilities and sometimes your life. They will sometimes be accurate and sometimes unfair, but they will always be there to report to the world just what their impressions of you are as a person, as a driver, and as a team player. Remember that their impressions may differ from your opinion, but their impressions are what will paint a picture for the many thousands that you will come into contact with throughout your career. The media people you meet on the way up will also more than likely be around for all facets of your career.

Your traits, personality, strengths, and weaknesses are the truth about you, and the only thing that does not change is the truth.

EARLY PERSONAL RELATIONSHIPS

In 1965, the first motor race I saw as a young boy (12 years old) in my hometown of Dublin, Ireland, featured an English driver named Morris "Mo" Nunn. Thirteen years later, I made my Formula One debut driving the Ensign Grand Prix car for the same Mo Nunn. More than 35 years later, I still worked with Mo as I gathered information for my television duties featuring his Champ Car and IRL race teams.

In 1969, when a young Brazilian hot shot named Emerson Fittipaldi moved to England to develop his racing career, he started by racing in a Merlyn Formula Ford. Midway through the season, he was in the Lotus Formula Three team, and by the end of the year, he was the British Formula Three champion. His two teammates were Dave Walker, the Australian who would partner Emerson just three years later in his first world championship–winning season, and Morris Nunn, who two decades later would engineer the Brazilian's Indy car to a CART Champ Car championship win and an Indy 500 win. Both Emerson and Mo Nunn are good friends of mine today and willing resources when I do television work.

At a street circuit in Dunboyne, Ireland, in 1965, I was introduced to an Irish race car driver named Sidney Taylor. Twelve years later, I was on the pole for the Formula Three support race for the Austrian Grand Prix when Sid Taylor walked up to my mentor, Derek McMahon, and promised that if I won the race, he would give me a test in a Formula One car. I won the race and less than six months later, Sid was true to his word, as he put me into a brand-new design of Formula One car: the Theodore, built by Australian Ron Tauranac at Ralt racing cars.

In 1968, Ireland's only permanent motor racing facility, Mondello Park, opened for its first race meeting. I boarded a bus in Dublin City for the 35-mile trip. Unbeknownst to me, the track was 5 miles beyond the end of the bus route. At the end of the day, I avoided the 5-mile walk back to the bus stop by hitching a lift from someone with a single-seat race car on an open trailer. It turned out to be businessman Frank Keane, who would become Ireland's BMW importer, and who also helped sponsor me in the European Formula Two championship . . . 10 years later.

MEMORABLE IRISH MEETING

While I struggled to race in Ireland in 1975, I became aware of a large (about 300 pounds of large) Irish businessman named Derek McMahon. Derek was affectionately known as "Big D." He raced successfully at a club level in Ireland and England and was a significant figurehead in Irish motorsports. Big D was well known for the amount of alcohol he could drink in a day and still be as fresh as a daisy the next day—even with limited sleep.

During a race meeting in Kirkistown (near Belfast, Northern Ireland), I heard that Big D was holding court at the bar. With my heart in my mouth, I summoned enough strength to approach him and ask if he would be interested in financially helping a young Irish driver who wanted to go to England and attempt to race professionally. He paused for a few seconds, swallowed hard, wiped his nose and face, looked at me a little sideways, and blurted out, "Listen here, young monkey, I need you like I need a f%#@&*# six-inch hole in me head."

With that response, I left with the proverbial tail between the legs. I left for England the next season and went on to win 23 Formula Ford races. At the end of the year, I managed to win the biggest event of the season, the Formula Ford Festival. It was a great season, but there did not seem to be any clear road forward because I did not have the financial wherewithal to continue.

I was planning for my return home to Ireland, when out of the blue I got a call from Big D. He asked me to meet him at the Dorchester Hotel in London, where he was attending the British Racing Drivers' Club (BRDC) end-of-season banquet. I walked in feeling like a fish out of water. That night, Big D said that he remembered my conversation of a year ago (even as short as it was) at the bar in Kirkistown, and he had followed my progress since then. He said he was impressed by my desire and commitment, and he would financially back me in the British Formula Three championship.

That relationship changed the direction of my life. Together, we won the British Formula Three championship in our first year. Big D became my mentor and sponsor and backed me all the way to Formula One. Thirty-one years later, I still call Big D and enjoy conversations about what we did together.

In 1977, I first came across McLaren International Chairman Ron Dennis when I was competing in my first Formula Two event in Estoril, Portugal. As a rookie, I had out-qualified both of his drivers—Italian-American Eddie Cheever and Brazilian Ingo Hoffman—and Dennis, in disbelief, came to my pit and told my team manager, "If Daly did that time, I'll eat my hat." The next day, I went even faster, and that was enough for Dennis to take note; he signed me to drive for his team for the 1979 season. I became established in Formula One for the 1980 season, after winning the last race I did for Dennis in the European Formula Two championship at Donnington Park, England. Dennis went on to build the hugely successful McLaren Formula One team and, 25 years later, I still work with him for my television duties.

While living in England in 1976, I met and became friends with Ian Phillips, the editor of *Autosport*. Phillips had a desire to help young drivers make their way through the clutter of motorsports, and we had many discussions about what I should do and how I should try to do it. Because Phillips was the editor of the most significant motorsports magazine in England, he was a good resource for someone like me to learn about the people and places that might be able to help me develop my career. Many times, I would not have the funds to spend on a hotel room for the night, and I would sleep on Phillips' couch in London, with his dog, Enzo. Enzo was a beautiful Golden Labrador named after Enzo Ferrari.

Unfortunately for me, he had total freedom in the house, and his favorite place to sleep was also on the couch, as the hair balls confirmed. Dog or no dog, it was a cheap place for me to get some sleep.

Twenty-seven years later, I wanted to do a television show about my experience track testing the Jordan Formula One car at Silverstone in England. Speed Channel in America had agreed to broadcast the show, and I put a production crew together using contacts in America and England. The person who provided me with total access to the Jordan team and who signed off on the project was none other than Ian Phillips, who was at that time in charge of business development at Jordan Grand Prix.

In 1982, Keke Rosberg and I drove for the Williams Formula One Team. Rosberg became world champion that year, and 20 years later, his son Nico, who just won the Formula BMW championship in Germany, tested the Williams BMW. After winning the GP2 championship in 2005, Nico was signed to be a full-time grand prix driver for Williams. Don't think for a minute that Keke Rosberg's ongoing friendship/relationship with Frank Williams did not pave the way for the initial test and then the contract to race.

In 1976, I moved from Ireland to England to race Formula Fords. One of the strongest cars I had to race against was the Royale. The Royale factory was forever developing new parts and ideas. The Royale designer in those days was a little-known

South African designer called Rory Byrne, with whom I developed a friendship and for whom I have a great respect. More than 25 years later, our friendship is just as strong, although Rory has been a little busy designing the Ferraris that carried Michael Schumacher to five of his seven world championships.

During those heady days of Formula Ford in England, one of my friends and close competitors was John Bright (who drove one of the very special Rory Byrne–designed Royales). Thirty years later, we had a discussion in the paddock in Daytona about how to get my son Conor to England to help develop his young racing career.

When I moved to England in 1976, I was introduced to Alan Henry and Peter Windsor. They were regarded as two of the best journalists of their day and wrote many stories about me during my career in Formula One. Thirty years later, I still work with both of them on American Formula One television broadcasts.

Whether it is Alonso, Andretti, Bourdais, Button, Earnhardt, Gordon, Raikkonen, or Tracy, you will find that all drivers have similar stories about long-term relationships. However, you will find that the great drivers have been able to develop substantial relationships that usually end up paving the way for them to take significant steps throughout their careers. As great a driver as Michael Schumacher was, he also needed a little help from his friends. In 1990, his relationship with Mercedes sports car team owner Peter Sauber was such that he paid for his first Formula One drive with the Jordan team.

These are just a few examples highlighting the fact that motorsports is a small, relationship-driven family. One of the first things I say to young drivers is to get out and meet and mix with the people you want to race. Get to the races, roam the pit lanes, and introduce yourself to the principals. I remember having to do that when I started out, and I was really bad at it. Because I was basically shy, I had to force myself to do it. That wasn't easy, but some of those relationships endure today.

There is a good and a bad side to a relationship-driven business. If you burn bridges, it will more than likely come back to haunt you. Burning bridges can also highlight a personality trait that some teams just would not want to deal with. On the flip side, by building and enhancing friendships and relationships, it can lead to more career breaks and sponsorship. Successful teams are the result of the collective strengths of teams of people working together in harmony and growing together through the good and bad days.

BACKGROUND

I was one of the very fortunate people who got to live my dream. I came from a working-class family in Dublin, Ireland. My father made his living first as a meat salesman and eventually as the owner of a corner grocery store. I grew up in an average neighborhood, where we played soccer and amused ourselves with some of the simpler things of life. I was always mechanically minded, became interested in motorsports at an early age, and clearly remember having to call our local newspaper to find out the results of Formula One races because they were not covered by television (or even newspapers) at that stage. No one in our neighborhood knew anything about motorsports, as it was a sport that was for the "other people."

In 1965, when I was 12 years of age, I saw my first race on the streets of Dunboyne, a small village on the outskirts of Dublin. My dad drove me the 35 miles from our house to watch Saturday practice, but I had to ride my bicycle out on Sunday because my dad was not available. Dunboyne was a typical Irish village with a grocery store, Catholic church, graveyard, and five or six pubs. It featured narrow roads, and its signature section was a humpback bridge that claimed the lives of two drivers that weekend. Because of those deaths, 1965 was to be the last year ever for street racing in Dunboyne.

That weekend of sitting on the grass bank with soggy sandwiches in my backpack changed the course of my life. The sights, the noise, and the smells captivated me so much that the day set me on a path I would follow for the rest of my life. I went to watch Sidney Taylor, the brother of one of my dad's grocery store customers. Taylor had a white Brabham BT 8 that he sometimes shared with future Formula One world champion Denny Hulme. Taylor had come to Ireland from England with his race transporter and was staying with his sister in our neighborhood. When I came home from school, there was an extra sense of excitement because my dad had arranged for me to see the race car inside the transporter. I still remember climbing up into the driver's seat and looking back at the white Brabham with the green stripe and the Irish shamrock symbol on the bonnet.

Driving in the Formula Libre event that day in Dunboyne was Mo Nunn, who 13 years later would give me my Formula One debut at Brands Hatch, England, in his Ensign MN08 DFV Formula One car. Although I have photos of Nunn that day, he was not one of the standouts, and I have no memory of his participation.

My own competition career started in 1969, when I made my debut in what we called stock car racing in Santry Stadium, Dublin, driving an old Ford Anglia E93A I had acquired unexpectedly. One Sunday morning while attending the stock car races in Santry Stadium, I met a man called Jack Murphy, who had raced the Ford Anglia but had blown the engine. The car lay on the side of the road with a replacement engine sitting in the boot. I paid him $15, and my dad towed the car home on the end of a rope. My parents contributed to my career through encouragement, with an overload of moral and emotional support.

I was 16 years old at the time and rode my Yamaha 50cc motorcycle to school every day. To get the money to race, even at such a low entry level, I needed to work. While I worked at the local gas station, my dad fitted the replacement engine, and my racing career was about to start. Before I appeared at the track, I had to give my new race car a new look. I scoured the tool shed at home for whatever house paint was left over, and my "Thunderbird" was created using the basic color scheme of a typical 1960s home.

The track was a small dirt oval that promoted racing as a full-contact sport . . . hence the steel bars around the cars. We couldn't afford a trailer, and Irish law at that time didn't allow me to drive on the road until I was 18, so my dad had to tow the Anglia on the end of a rope across the city to the track where my life's learning curve began.

Over the next five years, through the dust and dirt of Santry Stadium, I won countless races and championships before the time came to move on.

My road racing career began in 1974 at the wheel of a used Lotus 61 Formula Ford, purchased from Jordan Grand Prix team owner Eddie Jordan. I was 21 years old, a young race driver at that time. On my first test day, when we towed the car to the circuit with a rope, my run resulted in a crash through the trees that practically bent the car in half. That night at home, I could hardly walk because of the pain in my right leg. I didn't dare tell my mother about that!

To get the budget to race in Ireland that year, I had my dad sign for a loan at the local bank on the pretense of opening a used car business. I didn't believe that the bank manager needed to know that the used car in question was a used race car. I figured that I needed the money to have any sort of chance of success, and if it didn't work out, I had a lifetime to pay it back.

I had progressed to having an open trailer at that stage, but the cars I towed with were a little on the sketchy side. Road racing success came quickly for me, as I won a variety of public road hillclimbs, and I actually managed to win my fifth-ever road race, in the wet, at our local track, Mondello Park. To supplement my income, I worked at a local car repair shop where I could also prepare the race car.

AUSTRALIAN IRON-ORE LABORER

At the end of that season, I had not repaid the bank loan and needed more money to upgrade my race equipment for the 1975 season. The only options I was aware of to make big money, fast, during the winter, were to work in the oil fields of Alaska or the iron-ore mines of Australia. The Alaskan oil fields required special warm clothing that cost almost $1,000, and that expense would be taken from my pay packet every month until paid back. Australia required old T-shirts and shorts, so, five days after I found out about the opportunity, I was in Perth, committing to be a laborer in the iron-ore mines of northwest Australia.

It was an amazing odyssey. The other dreamers and I were put on a small plane in Perth that headed straight north. As we swooped in for landing, I was scouring the ocean waters for sharks. When we exited the plane onto the dirt runway, we were greeted by 90-degree heat, blazing sunshine, and flies . . . lots of flies. We were packed into the back of an open truck and driven across the dirt roads of the bush to what we soon would know to be "singlemen's quarters." Until there was a room available in the town, we had to live in wooden buildings in rooms that were approximately 10 feet by 6 feet. This would be my home for the next six months and the next step to chasing the dream.

Cliffs Robe River mining town in Wickham, northwest Australia, was the scene of the hottest, dirtiest, and hardest work I had ever done in my life. We mixed with the roughest class of humanity, who thought nothing of settling an argument with a knife or a gun.

The key to making big money in the iron-ore mines was the number of hours you could put in during a two-week period. On payday, every other Friday, fellow dreamers would gather in the food mess hall to see how many hours were booked. The first eight-hour shift paid the regular hourly rate, the second eight hours paid double time, but if you could work 24 hours straight, the final eight hours would pay triple time. That was the aim for many of the more determined.

There were people from all walks of life there with different reasons for needing cash. Some wanted to buy houses, some wanted to pay off debt, many were drug addicts who needed to feed their habits, and one in particular, Richard Burgess, was there to finance the purchase of a yacht.

There was a local dirt track, called Roeborne Raceway, in a neighboring town. Naturally, I attended as often as possible and convinced some friends to let me have a go several times. It was more dirt racing, but my focus was really on road racing.

After six months of toil, sweat, and fun digging iron ore, I returned to Ireland with $10,000. It was more money than I had ever had before. The dirt of the mines gave me the chance to purchase a used Crossle 25F Formula Ford race car from my best friend, Gary Gibson. The iron-ore laborer was ready to continue his racing career in 1975.

LIFTOFF

The 1975 season was a classic—I won most of the significant races in Ireland, setting most of the lap records and winning the Irish Formula Ford championship. However, it didn't go according to plan initially. My new (to me) race car was almost good enough to win. I was almost on the pace, but, at my local track, Mondello Park, I destroyed it in a big crash midway through the season. At that stage, I thought my career was over, as I had spent most of the Australian money. While we surveyed the wreck on the open trailer, the owner of the Crossle car company, John Crossle, walked up to me and offered to take the wreck in exchange for a brand-new, state-of-the-art Crossle 30F. John Crossle had obviously regarded me as a driver who might be able to win some races in his car, and therefore other people might buy more cars. This was to be the first significant break of my career. Armed with the brand-new car, I dominated the second half of the season and won just about everything, including the Irish championship.

LEAVING HOME

For the 1976 season, I got upgraded to racing internationally in England. My personal wealth (which was mainly tied to the worth of my race car) enabled me to either race or live reasonably, but I could not do both at the same time. As racing was the priority, I bought an old school bus, removed the seats, cut the back out, built two wooden ramps, and rolled my Formula Ford inside my mobile home and workshop. The toolbox sat on one side, the race car was in the middle, and the sleeping bag was on the other side. I said goodbye to my family, goodbye to my homeland, and went on to win 23 races, including the most prestigious end-of-season Formula Ford event of the year, the Tribute to James Formula Ford Festival. The 1976 FF Festival was so-named to honor England's reigning Formula One World Champion, James Hunt. James presented me with the trophy while my entire family was present. This was a very proud moment for me.

In 1977, the rocket ship really started to take off. Armed with financial backing from Irish businessman Derek McMahon, better known as "Big D," and a Chevron B38

Toyota Formula Three car, I started to pursue the British Formula Three championship. The British Formula Three championship was always, and indeed still is, regarded as the most prestigious F3 championship in the world. Any driver who won that championship, or who showed really well, went to Formula One. Formula One drivers who have followed this path include: Jenson Button, David Coulthard, Johnny Herbert, Eddie Irvine, Jonathan Palmer, Nelson Piquet, Ayrton Senna, and Derek Warwick.

That season was one of extremes: tears and joy all within the space of a few races. Racing was simpler back then, and we didn't have the large transporters, team managers, and engineers found on a modern team. We ran with one mechanic, who was the team manager, chief mechanic, gopher, and engineer all rolled into one. We converted a small van and ran the car inside on some wooden planks mounted on concrete blocks. We towed a small caravan (trailer) behind. We had just one car, one spare engine, and no spare parts.

Midway through the season, it all began to come together. Although I had yet to win a race, at the British Grand Prix support race, I led for many laps before crashing out with my arch rival, Stephen South. I practically cried after the race when I tried to explain what happened to Big D. Two weeks later, at the Austrian Grand Prix Formula One race, the support event again was for Formula Three cars. The circuit was the famous Osterreichring, the fastest circuit I had ever been on. I was on the pole with future three-time Formula One world champion Nelson Piquet beside me in the front row. We were combatants in the British championship, but this was the most prestigious event in which either of us had ever competed.

Just before the start, Irishman Sid Taylor (the same Sid Taylor I had watched race in Ireland in 1965), who handled Hong Kong–businessman Teddy Yip's Formula One involvement, walked up to my mentor, Big D, and told him that if I won the race, he would give me a Formula One test at the end of the season.

After a classic Formula Three battle between Piquet and me, I won the race that day and went on to win the last five races in a row back in England, as well as the British championship. It was a fairy-tale ending that I thought could only happen to other people . . . and it was happening to me.

The run of success at the end of that season in England started at Brands Hatch, and as I came down the stairs from the victory podium, I met a surprise visitor to the track. Richard Burgess, who I had shared many a night shift with in the iron-ore mines of Australia, was there to greet and congratulate me. Burgess had arrived in England on board the yacht that he bought with the proceeds of his days as a laborer in the iron-ore mines of Australia. What joy we had that season.

Toward the end of the season, I received a call from Guy Edwards. Edwards was regarded as the premier procurer of sponsorship in motorsports. He had helped fund many teams in the European Formula Two championship, as well as some Formula One teams. Guy inquired if I would be interested in driving his ICI-sponsored Chevron Formula Two car at Estoril, Portugal, in the penultimate round of the European Formula Two championship. Big D again stepped up with sponsorship funding, and I was ready to take the next step up the ladder.

I had never seen the car before and hadn't seen the track until the first lap I did in practice. After the first qualifying session, McLaren Chairman Ron Dennis (he owned a Formula Two team at the time called Project Four) walked into our pit in disbelief at my lap time and said, "If Daly did that lap time, I'll eat my hat."

In the next session, I went even faster and blew off his drivers, Italian-American Eddie Cheever and Brazilian Ingo Hoffman. I had a spectacular weekend, finishing in fifth place and having set a new lap record that stood for six years, until the Grand Prix returned to the track in 1984. Guy Edwards, who was an ex–Formula One driver and who then concentrated on acquiring sponsorship for teams, was sufficiently impressed to become my manager.

FORMULA FORD TO FORMULA ONE IN 13 MONTHS

In December 1977, just as he had promised, Sid Taylor gave me a test in a brand-new Theodore Formula One car at Goodwood, one of the most famous old circuits in England. The car had just been designed and built by Ron Tauranac. The

F1 project had been financed by Teddy Yip, for whom I would drive the following year. Yip was one of the principal backers of Mo Nunn's Team Ensign.

I had gone from Formula Ford to Formula One in 13 short months. Emerson Fittipaldi had achieved the feat in 18 months. It was an awesome accomplishment that I did not fully appreciate at the time. I was a typical young, hungry, invincible driver, unaware of anything outside of my immediate environment.

I sailed easily through the lower formulae, but when I got to Formula One, that vital momentum seemed to desert me. I began to struggle, and things just did not keep going my way. Finishing well was much more difficult. I tried very hard and began to make mistakes at critical times.

I was driven by the stopwatch and not by how the car felt. I drove for some great teams, such as Tyrrell and Williams, but squandered the opportunities. I was out of synch, and instead of controlling my own destiny with proactive decisions, I was becoming reactive to my environment. I had a great opportunity to score my first world championship points at the Austrian Grand Prix in the Ensign, but I made a small mistake toward the end of the race, spun off the road, and threw it away.

My first real break came when Ken Tyrrell showed up at the last round of the European Formula Two championship in Donington, England, in 1979. Tyrrell was interested in me as his driver for the following season. He liked what he saw in Donington (I won from the pole) and offered to run a third car for me at the last two Formula One races of the 1979 season: Watkins Glen and Montreal. The audition went well (although I did throw away fourth-place points with a mistake toward the end of the race in Watkins Glen), and I was signed for the 1980 season.

The season went well until I made a big mistake in Monaco going into the first corner. I braked too late and did two cartwheels through the air, taking out myself, Prost, Bruno Giacomelli, and my teammate, Jean Pierre Jarier. I then proceeded to get involved in a rash of crashes toward the end of the year that really shook my confidence. The crash at Monaco was my fault entirely, but at Zandvoort, I had a front brake disc explode. In Montreal, I got caught up in the Jones-Piquet squabble at the first chicane, and in Watkins Glen, I was attacked from behind by the wayward Andrea de Cesaris.

I lost the drive at the end of the year and moved over to the March team. This also started off badly, as I failed to qualify for the first six Grand Prix races of the year. I did not have a strong enough foundation to fall back on, and the struggle went on for years. My next break came in Formula One when I joined the great Williams Grand Prix team in 1982. Frank Williams was aware of me because I had won the British Formula Three title, and I had shown flashes of potential with a variety of

Formula One teams. Also, his choices were limited, as the established stars were already contracted to other teams.

Williams did not have the fastest car that year, but the team had the most reliable car and one that was fast enough to make a difference. At the end of 1980, I married my childhood sweetheart, Siobhan Ryan, and even that relationship became a burden to me because I was not equipped to understand or handle it. I had flashes of brilliance all through the 1982 season, but I never connected the dots and never drove with the flair and ease that I had in the lower formulae. The first time out in Zolder at the Belgian Grand Prix, I again threw away fourth-place points with a mistake toward the end of the race. At the Dutch Grand Prix, I was lapped by my teammate after a terrible race.

The defining moment of the season came when I was leading the Grand Prix of Monaco. While rounding the La Rascasse hairpin to start the last lap, my Williams stopped without any drive. The drive was lost because I had wiped the rear wing off in a half spin at Tabac corner while charging toward the front of the field. The oil cooler for the gearbox was mounted on the rear wing. As the gearbox pumped the oil, it went out onto the racetrack until there was none left to lubricate the gearbox, which eventually failed.

It was another error that proved very costly. For the rest of the season, I failed to put any consistent performances together and made too many mistakes. At the end of the year,

Frank Williams fired me. To top that off, after two years of marriage, I went through a divorce. Those two events really knocked me sideways.

AMERICA, THE LAND OF CURIOSITY

At the end of the 1982 Formula One season, Frank Williams phoned to let me know that Jacques Lafitte would be replacing me in the Williams FW08C for the upcoming season. I didn't blame him one bit, as I knew full well that I had not performed well enough to keep my seat. Soon after that, I left for America to start the next phase of my career among the high-speed ovals of American Indy car racing.

My first race was organized by Jeff Hutchinson, a journalist and friend, and Ted Quackenbush, an agent. I arrived in Phoenix, Arizona, in October 1982 to see the car and meet the team. Coming from the world of Formula One, I was shocked by what I found. The team was owned by enthusiasts Herb and Rose Wysard, who ran a 200-mile-per-hour race car at a standard lower than I had run Formula Ford cars in Ireland. It looked so shabby I joked with Ted that I needed a tetanus injection to sit in the thing. The first time I pressed the throttle pedal, it stayed on the floor. Apparently, the previous driver, John Paul Junior, had gone off the road and punched the floor up into the throttle pedal assembly, and that jammed the pedal. No one had bothered to fix it. After much soul-searching, I decided to try to race it to at least get a feel for what oval-track racing was all about. I qualified ninth beside American Johnny Rutherford, but the engine blew up halfway around the first lap.

I made my Indianapolis 500 debut in 1983, and in September 1984 I was almost killed in a devastating crash at the Michigan International Speedway. I somehow survived an approximately 210-mile-per-hour impact—the hardest impact that anyone had survived up to that time.

I was driving for Tony Bettenhausen's Provimi Veal–sponsored team, and we were struggling to find the speed of the front-runners. My first laps at the Michigan International Speedway were jaw-dropping to say the least. The first time, I went flat-out into turn one, and the g forces created by the high banks were so strong that my helmet was literally pushed down on my head so much that it partially covered my eyes. It was hard to believe that a car traveling that fast could somehow go around what was in effect a 180-degree corner.

About 20 laps into the race, I was lapping at 219 miles per hour—faster than I had qualified. The track had a bump going into turn three, and every time the car would go over the bump, it would bounce up slightly, then settle down with an increased grip level on the right rear, and the car powered through the corner flat out from there. It was a rhythm that was repeated every lap. Lap after lap, the same feel from the car would be transmitted to me, and I felt as if I was just on the edge of adhesion.

On lap 26, it all went wrong. A slight mist began to fall, and the grip level was reduced as the car landed on the other side of the bump. Rather than dig in and stick, the tire slid, and the car began to spin. It spun so fast that it threw my head back against the headrest. I realized I was in big trouble and clearly remember saying to myself, "Oh shit." I remember pulling my legs back as far as I could into the cockpit.

I have no memory of what happened in the next 15 seconds or so. Even when I look at the photos, it's hard to connect my memories of the crash with the destruction. The car hit with such blunt force that it literally exploded. The front of the car, including the dashboard bulkhead and half of the cockpit, broke off. I was left strapped to the back half of the tub without any frontal protection and with my body exposed to a second and potentially fatal impact against the outside wall.

John Paul Junior decided that for him to miss the crash he would go high on the banking in an attempt to drive around the carnage. His decision saved my life because as he arrived on the scene, I was a few feet from the wall and still doing over 100 miles per hour. He hit me broadside, lifted my car clear off the ground, and spun me down toward the infield. Within minutes, the mist had turned to rain, and the race was cancelled for the day.

About two seconds before the wreck stopped rolling down off the banking, I was alert again. I was dazed but felt no pain. I took a mental inventory to see which parts of my body I could feel. Legs, OK, torso, OK, right hand, OK . . . but a chill ran through my body when I realized I couldn't feel my left arm.

I immediately thought that I had suffered the same fate as my team manager, Merle Bettenhausen, who had his left arm severed in a similar accident at Michigan. I used my right hand to grab through the face mask of my helmet and pull my head down enough to see that my left arm and hand were still attached but severely burnt and covered in blood.

The head of Championship Auto Racing Team's (CART) safety team, Dr. Steve Olvey, arrived and knelt down in front of me, and he directed the team as he stared into my eyes. Steve Edwards then leaned over and talked to me. Just as Edwards got up to attend the clean-up, I reached up and grabbed him by his collar and, in a scared, broken voice, pleaded with him not to leave me. I was terrified.

I suffered severe orthopedic injuries to my left ankle, left leg, hip, ribs, and pelvis, and had a toe amputated in the accident. I had a lacerated liver, mild head injuries, and very painful third-degree burns on my left arm. I was in intensive care in the University of Michigan hospital for a week before being transported via a medical emergency flight service to Methodist Hospital in Indianapolis. I required multiple surgeries, including bone and skin grafts, over the following two years, followed by about four years of physical therapy. The accident rocked my world and changed my views on many things.

I wanted to continue racing and every day was dedicated to becoming physically and mentally as strong as possible. I was back in a race car for the following year's Indy 500 even though I had to use a cane to actually walk.

During my recovery period, I became more and more interested in television broadcasting. In 1985, I signed a contract with America's best-known sports cable channel, ESPN. That contract was to last for the next 10 years, with me covering everything from Formula Ford to Formula One. In addition to my racing career, I began to travel the world for television duties.

I also spent a great deal of my time studying drivers and pondering why some drivers, with what seemed to be similar driving talent, managed to achieve more success than others. There appeared to be some traits that the champions possessed, and I began to study what they were.

I went back to racing full-time in mid-1987 but was never as good a driver again. I could not mentally bring myself to my pre-accident state. Losing the edge I needed to win prompted me to delve a little deeper into how I could improve as a driver. I won the biggest international races of my career—the 1990 and 1991 Sebring 12-hour races—before I retired in 1992.

To my surprise, I would learn more about what I needed to compete after I retired from active competition.

REALITY CHECK

My near-fatal accident put me on a learning path that I hope can positively influence others. It was years after I retired from competition that I realized drivers have strengths and, more importantly, weaknesses. I had not recognized my own weaknesses while I was driving, and therefore I had not worked at turning those weaknesses into strengths. My personal experiences are a valuable asset that I can now pass on to the next generation of race drivers, and I will get a great deal of satisfaction from seeing them succeed.

Throughout my career as a race car driver, I was always deeply involved in what I was doing at that particular time, and I did not focus very much on what made the difference between winning and losing. Naturally, I was so focused that I believed my strengths were enough to carry me through, and I ignored my weaknesses. In fact, I never recognized or admitted that I had any weaknesses. Perhaps I was too arrogant or afraid that if any weakness was ever exposed, it might somehow stall my progress. The reality is that every team manager knew of my weaknesses, and I now know that exposing weakness early in my career would have made me a much more effective driver and could have changed the way my career developed. This is a large part of what I want young drivers to realize with the help of this book.

For many years, while I competed in Formula One, Indy cars, and World Sport cars, I had ample opportunity to race against and mix socially with some of the best drivers in the world. I was part of a great era of drivers, including Mario and Michael Andretti, Emerson Fittipaldi, Niki Lauda, Nigel Mansell, Rick Mears, Ronnie Peterson, Nelson Piquet, Alain

Prost, Bobby Rahal, Johnny Rutherford, Jody Scheckter, Al Unser, and Gilles Villeneuve.

While in the television booth, I closely observed great drivers/champions, such as Fernando Alonso, Michael and Mario Andretti, Sébastien Bourdais, Gil de Ferran, Dale Earnhardt, Jeff Gordon, Nelson Piquet, Alain Prost, Michael Schumacher, Ayrton Senna, Tony Stewart, and Alex Zanardi. Although each driver has strengths and weaknesses, they have all consistently shown that they possess the abilities not only to drive a car fast, but also to create and manage their respective environments, which can potentially put them in a position to be consistently successful. Note that I say *potentially* put them in a position to be consistently successful. As you go through this book, you will realize that some of them almost get to the top, and some of them might never get there.

What is it that separates the consistent winners from the pretenders? What is it that makes some drivers special? Why do some drivers become champions and others never reach their potential? Ultimately, this book will answer that question. The answer has the potential to send you on the road to stardom by detailing clearly what you need in order to develop the skills to become a true champion.

Throughout this book, I will give examples of current and past star drivers in an effort to clearly show the differences between drivers who have all the key elements and drivers who do not possess all the elements. As often as I can, I will use real-life scenarios in an effort to paint a clear picture of the often-subtle differences between having the skills and almost having them. I will use documentation from respected journalists who follow every step these drivers take, and you will probably see yourself in some of the examples. Remember, you can still make it to the top without all the elements fully developed, but you will not have the maximum staying power possible. With all the ingredients fully developed, you will sustain your position at the top.

Becoming a champion is not a game of chance, but it can be a game of choice. If you develop the Champion's Pyramid as much as you possibly can, you might not become a world champion, but you will definitely become the very best you can be. What more can you ask for?

CHAPTER 2

TALENT IDENTIFICATION

Do you possess a predominantly instinct-reflex talent, is it a feel-sensitive talent, or is it a combination of both?

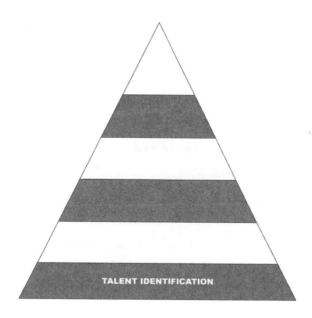

TALENT IDENTIFICATION

In 1995, CART Champ Car team owner Barry Green from Team Green asked the Derek Daly Performance Driving Academy in Las Vegas to create an American driver-development program on behalf of tobacco giant Brown & Williamson. We had the opportunity to work with 46 of the most talented young drivers in America over a three-year period.

Racing drivers' styles vary as widely as their personalities and appearance. Working with them was a fascinating exercise that quickly exposed the strengths and weaknesses of each driver. The drivers had to attend our academy alone, without the immediate moral support of family or friends. Within hours of starting the course, each driver's profile began to emerge during the exercises with which we challenged them—they could not hide anything from us.

As the program progressed, some drivers were intimidated, some used the book of excuses, and others welcomed the opportunity and relished the competition.

Some drivers went fast immediately, and some took their time to get comfortable. Some drivers coped with adversity well, and some got flustered. To do the same lap times, some got there aggressively using more tires, brakes, and fuel; some got the lap times with ease and finesse. It was fascinating to see the different styles and approaches unfold in front of us.

After three days of initial evaluation, we knew the strengths and weaknesses of the drivers with real potential. We also realized that for each of the drivers to progress up the ladder to stardom, they would need individually tailored programs to suit their particular profiles.

Racing drivers, by their very nature, are ego-driven and are almost scared to think that someone would know that they have a weakness. This fear is the first big mistake that could derail a career. Truth and honesty in the early stages can create an unshakable foundation for a young driver. Just as the stop-watch never lies, the truth is the only thing that never changes.

Remember that nearly every young driver that I have worked with has a profile of strengths and weaknesses. Recognizing and developing those weaknesses is the key to building what we now know as the Champion's Pyramid. If we accept that every driver has God-given talent, one might assume that the strengths and/or weaknesses are technical, communicative (people skills), emotional, or mental in nature. However, as we delve into what type of God-given talent a driver might have, you begin to expose the foundation that must first be clearly understood.

Any potential racing star is born with an inherent ability to understand the dynamics of a vehicle at high speed. The driver has the ability to feel through his backside what a car will do before it does it (which is vital at a place like Indianapolis). He has a message delivery system from the butt cheeks to the brain and from the back to the arms and legs that is permanently connected. He *knows* that when a car slides, you steer into the slide to regain control. You can't teach this instinctive reaction. It's the same when something is about to hit you. Your natural instinct causes you to put your hands up to protect yourself. The reaction is instinctive; nobody taught you.

On this level, the important question is not whether you have talent, but rather what type of driving talent were you born with? Do you possess a predominantly instinct-reflex talent, is it a feel-sensitive talent, or is it a combination of both?

A driver who has instinct-reflex talent can drive the wheels off anything he gets into. No matter what the track conditions or car setup, this driver will extract the maximum speed possible out of the car. These drivers are not known for strong technical feedback. These are gifted drivers who are well-liked by a team because the team knows that every time the driver is in the car, the speed they extract is all the speed the car has. The downside is that the team must know how to set up the car to get its maximum speed. The driver is too busy driving hard and fast to feel what the car is doing, and therefore the driver does not lead the team technically.

Drivers that possess this kind of talent include Jean Alesi, A. J. Allmendinger, Robby Gordon, Mika Hakkinen, Tony Kanaan, Juan Montoya, and Kimi Raikkonen.

Drivers with primarily feel-sensitive talent are naturally attuned to what the car does and can accurately suggest the setup changes needed to go faster. Drivers who have primarily feel-sensitive talent include David Coulthard, Gil de Ferran, Sam

Hornish, Rick Mears, Dario Franchitti, Al Unser, Al Unser Jr., and Bobby Unser. These drivers can take bad cars and accurately identify the right changes necessary to engineer the car to go faster.

A few extraordinary drivers have a combination of both talent styles. These drivers have the ability to engineer a car to go faster and, when the car is not performing well, are still able to drive it as fast as it can go. Drivers known for this kind of multi-faceted talent include Fernando Alonso, Mario Andretti, Sébastien Bourdais, Cristiano da Matta, Dale Earnhardt Sr., Jeff Gordon, Michael Schumacher, Paul Tracy, and Alex Zanardi. According to BMW's Mario Thiessen, Poland's Robert Kubica also has both qualities.

INSTINCT-REFLEX DRIVERS

Instinct-reflex drivers have nerve endings that are on fire, and every fiber of their bodies is fully charged and ready to be unleashed as soon as they put on a helmet. Early in his career, an instinct-reflex driver becomes popular because he is usually a no-nonsense driver who gets the job done. He is hindered by few distractions and only thinks about going fast. Engineering the car to go faster is not a high priority for the instinct-reflex driver because that is not in his character. These drivers are often ego-driven and believe that regardless of the car setup, they are invincible. In the lower formulae, they can get away with this because going fast doesn't require a complicated setup. Races tend to be short and tires spec; therefore, a flat-out sprint driver can do quite well. As long as a team can provide the driver with a reasonable setup, he will happily do the rest.

Mika Hakkinen was fortunate to be a McLaren driver in a high-tech era when engineers and computers could provide a setup that best utilized his instinct-reflex style. The cars of the late 1970s and early 1980s required more accurate technical feedback from the driver, and I don't believe Hakkinen would have been as successful in 1970s-era Formula One.

Many think that one of Jean Alesi's biggest career mistakes was moving to Ferrari when he could have gone to Williams. Ferrari lured him through the emotional appeal, but the team did not provide him with cars good enough to take advantage of his phenomenal instinct-reflex style. Some think that Williams could have provided him with a better car at that time in his career. What Alesi needed to become a champion at that time was a team that could provide him with a good car with minimal input from the driver. In that type of environment, Alesi would have been more successful.

During race setup testing at the 2007 Indianapolis 500, Tony Kanaan was asked why Dario Franchitti was doing most of the driving. Tony said that Franchitti was pickier than he was. This statement indicates that Tony recognizes he is an instinct-reflex driver while Franchitti is a feel-sensitive driver.

Juan Montoya's career ended in Formula One because he was an instinct-reflex driver. He was paired with Kimi Raikkonen, another instinct-reflex driver. The two of them provided poor technical feedback, and the McLaren engineers had a hard time finding the best setups for the McLaren Formula One car. A downward spiral begins when the driver does not have a good car (which he shares responsibility for) and tries to drive harder, which leads to mistakes and ultimately to disaster.

The instinct-reflex driver can frustrate a team because no matter how hard he drives, he might be just a little off the pace. He never thinks hard enough about the car setup and relies too much on other people to control his destiny. Again, this is easier to get away with in the lower formulae. Many kart drivers are instinct-reflex drivers because they have tuners who set up their karts for them. This act, although well-intentioned by the parents who pay the tuners, can very often sabotage the future and long-term development of the driver.

What might be the signs that your driver is an instinct-reflex driver? Few pre-teen drivers understand more than the basics of push/understeer and loose/oversteer. When the driver is in his teen years, he does not really know what the car is doing when he drives it at high speed. In response to questions about the car, the driver may answer with a quick "Fine" or "OK."

When you delve a little deeper with probing questions, the young instinct-reflex driver will usually agree with whatever the engineer might say about how the car is handling. The parent and/or engineer must pay very close attention to these types of answers; the quicker you identify the talent type, the quicker the driver's style can be developed. Please remember, there is not a right or wrong type of inherent talent, but there is a right and wrong way to develop the driver. Instinct-reflex drivers need to be coached to pay more attention to the car and learn how to give better technical feedback. Tuners will always have to work harder with these drivers.

Another good way to get the most out of an instinct-reflex driver is to pair him with a good technical driver who can sort out the car. This not only helps the tuner with set-up, it also puts someone on the team from whom the instinct-reflex driver can learn.

FEEL-SENSITIVE TALENT

The drivers born with feel-sensitive talent can travel a similar path in their formative years, but they tend to have a bit more control of their destiny later in their careers because they have the ability to guide the team technically. A good feel-sensitive driver can drive a race car, absorb the message it is giving him, and accurately describe it to the engineers in enough detail that the engineer can almost feel as if he has driven the car himself. If you listen to the radio talk between a driver and engineer, the good feel-sensitive drivers clearly describe what the car is doing. They will also have an idea what direction to take with the setup.

A good feel-sensitive driver tends to think about the setup even when away from the track. It's part of his racing DNA to constantly think about improving his race car setup. If your driver talks to you during the week about things he feels with the car, it is a good indicator that he might be a feel-sensitive driver. A feel-sensitive driver might also use the word "feel" when describing the handling characteristics of the car.

"In the middle of the corner, I feel this," or, "on the rise in the back straight, I can feel the car do that," are typical statements made by a feel-sensitive driver.

Bear in mind that the feel-sensitive driver's quest for the perfect setup can get in the way of his ability to get in a car and drive it hard. The technical (feel) driver has to walk the fine line between knowing what he needs in the car and being fully prepared to give his all, even if the car is not perfect. Practice sessions are short on race weekends, and time to test is often limited.

The feel-sensitive driver can frustrate a team because he might not give his all if the car isn't perfect. Dario Franchitti and David Coulthard have a reputation for this behavior. Franchitti and Coulthard both have years of experience—they know exactly the type of tire and chassis setups that allow them to go fast. As these drivers gained experience, they became less likely to let it all hang out when the car lacked the feel that they liked. When the car is right, look out—these drivers will be as quick as anyone.

For the overall success of a team, it is vital for a driver and team owner/manager to understand exactly what type of talent their driver has and what part of the team needs to be supplemented to get the best results.

For example, one engineer might be enough for Sébastien Bourdais, Gil de Ferran, Mario Andretti, or Alex Zanardi because they are good at sorting out the right technical setup of the race car. Jean Alesi, Mika Hakkinen, and Juan Montoya need two or three engineers to make up for their inability to provide accurate technical feedback. All of these drivers have won some of the world's premiere races and championships. They did so when surrounded by the right elements. However, instinct-reflex drivers run the risk of wearing out their welcome with a team (Montoya at Williams and McLaren) if the team cannot find another way (other than from driver feedback) to develop the car.

THE MAGICAL COMBINATION

Drivers who possess both instinct-reflex and feel-sensitive talent are the most likely candidates to become champions with long careers at the very top of their profession. Naturally, this list of drivers tends to be shorter.

At the top of the list is Michael Schumacher. The masses might say that Schumacher won so many races because he had the best car. That is absolutely right. The cars he drove were the best because he is one of the most technically accurate feel-sensitive drivers ever to race in Formula One.

All through his Formula One career, no matter how the technical regulations changed, Schumacher could consistently lead a team in the right direction while developing the car. He was able to give good technical feedback from his earliest days in Formula One. His descriptions of how the car worked on the track were precise, vivid, and accurate. He made his car and team better, and that's why he had the best car so many times.

Former Formula One world champion Damon Hill also gave good technical feedback, and that ability put a championship-winning car at his disposal. I believe that Hill's Formula One career ended abruptly because Frank Williams did not fully understand his contribution on the technical side. Williams believed that a potentially faster driver would be more beneficial to the team, and he replaced Hill with Heinz-Harald Frentzen. When Damon Hill left, so did the technical direction of the team. Williams has not had a really fast car since. Damon Hill was not known for a flat-out banzai lap in qualifying, which would also put him in the feel-sensitive talent category.

Mario Andretti had both talents. He was regarded as a great technical driver that gave accurate feedback, and he also had the ability to drive on the ragged edge when it came time to really put it all on the line. His sustained high-performance ability is the true indicator that he had both.

Drivers with the magical combination of feel-sensitive and instinct-reflex talent tend to have more consistent performances. Using that measuring stick, you can see that Fernando Alonso, Mario Andretti, Sébastien Bourdais, Dale Earnhardt Sr., Jeff Gordon, Michael Schumacher, and Paul Tracy possess this combination. Drivers who have flashy performances, such as Dale Earnhardt Jr., Giancarlo Fisichella, Bruno Junqueira, and Jarno Trulli tend not to possess the combination.

DISCIPLINE OR LACK THEREOF

Now let's discuss the driver who has other tendencies. What about the driver who has good technical feel in the race car but does not have the discipline to concentrate on the setup work because all he wants to do is go fast? I know this type of driver very well because I was like this. I didn't know it at the time, but on reflection, it is now very obvious to me.

At the British Grand Prix on the weekend of my Formula One debut, my team owner and engineer was Mo Nunn of Ganassi, Zanardi, and Montoya fame. I drove the Ensign MN01, a very efficient F1 car that gave good feedback. After Friday's qualifying, I was in the top 15, and because of this, Goodyear rewarded us by allowing us to have a new-construction front tire for the final qualifying on Saturday. This tire would obviously help us stiffen up the front of the car and give us better traction. During the final one-hour session, with me trying to qualify for a Grand Prix for the first time, I did my first run on the old tires, and the lap times that resulted put me 12th on the grid. A ripple of excitement ran through our small team because the Ensign had not been to that end of the grid for a very long time.

The new-development front tires were then fitted, and out I went. They felt a lot stiffer, and the car's handling was oversteering (loose) as a result of excessive suspension roll at the front. Nunn was convinced that stiffening the roll bar would balance the car to allow me to take full advantage of the tires' benefits. I would not listen and insisted on running the old tires that I was familiar. I eventually qualified 15th and made my Grand Prix debut in front of my home crowd starting beside world champion James Hunt. Despite the fact that a rear wheel fell off midway through the race and I didn't finish, I was a hero for the day. Nevertheless, I often wonder what would have happened if I had had enough discipline not to be driven by the stopwatch and instead be driven by the car setup.

If the car is set up right, fast lap times just happen. I have come to believe that if I had been disciplined enough to listen to Nunn, my great grid position could have been even better, which might have prompted Goodyear to give us the better tires at the next race, and the rest of the season might have had a better foundation.

On the other side of this story, one of the most disciplined drivers I have ever seen is Al Unser Jr. He focused on the ultimate race setup and was able to resist the temptation to simply go fast. Unser's discipline during qualifying often led to him starting deep in the field, but in his heyday, he was consistently quick during the race. At the height of his career, Al Unser Jr. won the Long Beach Grand Prix five times in a row.

Another common flaw in a race driver is to spend too much time focused on the competition rather than on personal performance. After this type of driver runs, his first question is, "How fast were the other drivers?" Rather than concentrating deeply on his own performance, the driver is distracted by the performance of others. Remember to only expend energy on what you can control—your own performance. Forget the rest of the competition, because you cannot control them. Your performance is the only thing in your control that will affect the final outcome on race weekend. Not focusing on your personal performance is a major flaw, but it can be corrected. We will deal with this aspect of the driver's R-DNA in Chapter Five's examination of mental skills.

TEMPERAMENT

Now it is very important to remember that a driver's talent is just a part of his personal package. A driver's success is often a reflection of his talent, and how you deal with the driver in many situations is determined by his temperament. Drivers of all different temperaments succeed, and there is no link between temperament and success. The key is for the driver or, perhaps more importantly, the team manager to understand how to build an atmosphere around different drivers that suits their temperaments.

This topic will be covered in detail in the communication discussion in Chapter Four, along with breakdowns of the four basic temperaments and how to deal with the strengths and weaknesses of each.

One of the quietest, shiest racing drivers ever was Scotsman Jim Clark. He was also one of the greatest-ever drivers and became a Formula One world champion. Drivers who do not have a naturally outgoing personality need not fret because honesty and humility are also very endearing qualities.

Now that we've examined the distinctions between instinct-reflex and feel-sensitive talents, you should be able to see yourself in the examples given and have a basic understanding of what kind of driving talent you possess. You can also apply this analysis to your favorite drivers. Watch them on the track, in interviews, and on talk shows. How do they talk about the car? Can you figure out what kind of driver they might be? Can you see where some flourished in certain environments while others floundered?

When you closely examine just what type of talent you were blessed with, and if you are very honest with yourself, you can turn any weakness into a strength, but you must understand how to surround yourself with the right environment. If you do this, you can create a foundation for yourself that will stand tall for the rest of your career. Building that platform is a slow process, but you will have a better chance at a good payback if the foundation blocks are solid.

TYPICAL BEHAVIOR FOR DIFFERENT TYPES OF DRIVING TALENT

This chart will help you identify what kind of driver you are (or are coaching).

INSTINCT-REFLEX TALENT	FEEL-SENSITIVE TALENT
Responds to question, "How is the car?" with simple one-line answers	Responds to question, "How is the car?" with more detailed answers, often beginning with "I feel we need . . ."
Not sure of himself when talking about the car	Sure of car's needs
Talks in circles	Descriptive
Gets confused when challenged	Stick to guns on car performance
Inconsistent performances (wins one day, finishes 20th the next)	Consistent performances (top five even on an off day)
Test sessions can be a lottery	Test days productive
Not that interested in long debrief sessions	More interested in data and graphs
Team gets lost on setup often	Consistent setups
Close enough is good enough with seat position and other details	More particular about seat and pedal position
Media discussions tend to be from the heart	Media discussions more thoughtful and measured
Heavily influenced by the stopwatch	More disciplined during practice sessions
Drives 10/10ths (flat out) every lap	Drives 9/10ths during test sessions
Poor understanding of (or concern for) the information needed by the engineer or tuner	Excellent understanding of information needed by the engineer or tuner

ADVICE FOR EACH TYPE

INSTINCT-REFLEX DRIVER	FEEL-SENSITIVE DRIVER
Don't discuss car handling until you have had a little time to think about it	Give relevant info as soon as possible
Look at/understand setup sheets regularly	Give engineers/tuners room
Make sure that engineer/tuner tells you all changes to the car before you do each run (this helps the driver connect the changes made to the car with the feel difference)	Understand that feeling good might not always be the fastest way
Make an effort to pay attention in debrief sessions	Don't overanalyze in debriefs
Pay attention to the details	Don't look for perfection before performing at your highest level
Pay more attention during practice sessions	Don't always look for or expect perfection from the car
Drive at 9/10ths when testing	Drive at 10/10ths during qualifying, even when car is not perfect

CHAPTER 3

TECHNICAL SKILLS

It takes just as much time to bolt the wrong setup onto a race car as it does to bolt on the right one.

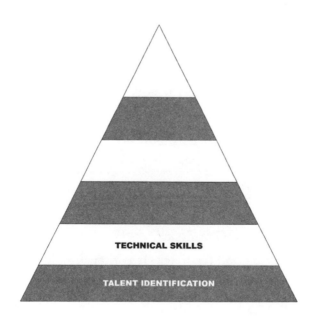

You do not have to be a good technical driver to drive a race car fast. For example, a pure instinct-reflex driver can set competitive lap times and even win a race here and there with little regard to race car setup. That's not the case, however, if you want to consistently win championships.

Why? Race cars have limits. In racing, the objective is to extract the car's maximum speed as often as possible. The key to sustained speed is to understand which changes to the car's setup will make it go faster. Most drivers can identify the handling, chassis, or engine issues that cause a race car to be slow. If a driver (and therefore the team) can come back from a practice or testing session and make suggestions that make the car faster, the team (and the driver) will be able to consistently be fast.

One of the most frustrating aspects of this is that most drivers' concepts of their abilities in this area are skewed. Drivers typically believe they have good technical feedback, and they would like others to also have the same opinion.

The importance of this skill is underscored by the way teams talk about new drivers. Next time you see an interview with a crew chief or owner after a test, watch what's said. If the test went well, you will invariably hear them say, "He did a great job, and he gave good feedback."

Teams love good feedback. It is their lifeblood. It makes their job much easier, and it makes the difference between winning and losing. It takes just as much time to bolt the wrong setup onto a race car as it does to bolt on the right one. The right setup will ultimately be guided by the driver and by what he says.

In the early days of racing, before the advent of contemporary data acquisition, technical feedback from a driver played a much more pivotal role than it does today. The driver (and lap times) was essentially the sole source of technical information about how the car was performing, from suspension and aerodynamics to engine performance and tire development. In today's world of electronic measuring devices that acquire data about the car's on-track performance and feed it into laptop computers in the pits, the driver's feedback direction is just as critical, but today the data gathered from these devices provides the team with enormous amounts of information in the form of graphs and printouts that can be cross-referenced with the driver's feedback.

Teams can get the car to perform at a fairly high level with the data acquisition and average feedback. In order to consistently run up front, however, a modern successful team requires precise, thoughtful feedback.

This smaller performance window is reflected in the grid times of today when compared to those of 10 or 15 years ago. When I first raced the Indianapolis 500 in 1983, the speed spread on the grid from fastest to slowest was 207 miles per hour (Teo Fabi) to 183 miles per hour (Chet Fillip). That equates to a time difference of about five seconds per lap.

The year before the split of open-wheel racing in America (1995) was the most competitive ever at Indy, where the speed spread from fastest to slowest was 231 miles per hour (Scott Brayton) to 225 miles per hour (Davy Jones). This was a time spread of just over one second per lap. When a grid is this close, the emphasis on good and accurate driver feedback becomes more critical.

Perhaps the most important aspect of car setup and testing is honesty. Honesty endears you to the team, and honesty is one of the most important foundation stones in building rapport with your team. Your instincts and seat-of-the-pants feel will tell you what to say to the engineers (or to your mechanic or helper).

When the Derek Daly Performance Driving Academy carried out the Team Green Academy driver-development program, there were instances during our evaluations when drivers were talking just for the sake of talking. Because they thought they should be saying something, they would try to show how much they knew instead of just dealing with the relevant facts. As soon as a driver begins to force the explanations and/or goes off on tangents during technical discussions, the antennas start to go up with the engineers, and questions and doubts about the driver's technical skills start to surface.

Never forget that a driver's style is unique to him, and therefore the required optimal setup is individual to that driver. A driver should not be looking to someone else to provide him with his setup. Often, in teams when one driver gets lost, a faster driver's setup will be bolted on, and the slower driver will go faster. This is a stop-gap measure for teams and drivers in trouble, but it can be effective if the slower driver uses the faster driver's setup as a starting point and fine-tunes it to suit his style.

No matter how you get the car on the right track, in the end, your technical setup has to suit your particular driving style. It is fundamentally wrong to try to make a driver change his style to suit a particular car or setup. There are elements of a driver's style that can be shaped differently, but his R-DNA will be tied directly to his natural driving style.

Some cars require a certain technique to make them go fast, but the final tuning of their chassis is individual to every driver. Just look at Michael Schumacher and his many teammates. Many of them tried to change their own styles of driving to mimic his because whatever Schumacher did was considered to be the fastest way. In changing their styles, most of his teammates went slower than they would have by sticking to their own styles.

Michael Schumacher always liked his cars predominantly stiffer than that of his teammates. His teammates inevitably got into trouble when they tried to use the stiffer setup he preferred. Former teammates, Martin Brundle, Johnny Herbert, Eddie Irvine, and Jean Alesi soon found out to their detriment that Michael's technical set was designed specifically for him.

When Rubens Barrichello tried to change from a right-foot braker to a left-foot braker to be more like Schumacher, he got temporarily lost and was just not fast. By the time the 2002 season came around, Barrichello had gone back to his natural left-foot style of braking and developed his own personal settings. To have the confidence to go your own way with car setup is vital. The changes suited him, and he again began to show his true talents (and speed). Barrichello was faster than Schumacher several times in 2002, and Schumacher incorporated some of his teammate's chassis settings.

It is much harder for some drivers than it is for others to test accurately and to steer a team in the right direction technically. Giving good feedback requires a driver to walk a fine line between seat-of-the-pants speed and chassis-feel discipline.

In test sessions, a driver should not drive at 10/10ths. When you drive at 10/10ths, you use all of your concentration. Driving at less than 100 percent allows you to pay closer attention to what the car is doing.

In addition to driving at less than maximum speed, a good test driver needs to turn consistent lap times, using the same braking points and lines. When you do this, changes made to the car are much easier to feel and you can offer meaningful comments about the results. The more talented the driver, the nearer the limit he can drive consistently during a test session.

ROOKIE TENDENCIES

Most rookie race car drivers are not technically feel-sensitive drivers and do not give good feedback. When you listen to their explanations about the race car, they often get mixed up as they talk. Very often, when testing with a new driver (and also with some experienced drivers), after a change is made to the car, he does a run and comes in and completely forgets what he was out there testing. This is a driver who is guided only by the stopwatch. I know this type of driver very well because I was one of them. I had these tendencies right through Formula One and into Champ Cars, and I had to literally talk to myself during test sessions to make sure that I focused on testing a setup rather than turning a faster lap.

The good technical drivers tend to be less emotional. They are much more methodical in their approach and the execution of their job. They are not any slower, just different.

STYLE DIFFERENCES

Champ Car champion Paul Tracy has an aggressive driving style. He is able to perform at his very best when he has a lot of front-end grip. When Bridgestone changed to a harder-compound Champ Car tire in 2001, Tracy struggled to find his blinding speed because he could not get the car to respond in the middle of the corners. When Team Green changed from a Reynard to the Lola for the third round of the 2002 championship in Japan, Tracy immediately topped the time sheets because the Lola has a much more positive front end, which suited his driving style.

The most important thing for Tracy, and any engineer that works with him, is to understand what his specific driving style needs to go fast.

GETTING TECHNICALLY LOST

An example of good drivers not being able to overcome a poor technical setup happened in the Japanese 2002 Champ Car race in Motegi with the Newman/Haas Racing team. With two of the best drivers in the series—Brazilians Cristiano da Matta and Christian Fittipaldi—their cars were so loose that 20 laps into the race, both da Matta and Fittipaldi looked like amateurs. Over the course of the race, they were lapped multiple times. The massive effort to transport all their equipment and team members halfway around the world was totally wasted because the right setup could not be found.

Those two showed their experience and ability to give good feedback later in the season at Chicago. Newman/Haas had completed enough testing—with accurate information from the drivers—to completely turn its oval-track performance around, and Cristiano da Matta stood on the top step of the podium as a proud winner.

During qualifying for the 1995 Indianapolis 500, Team Penske fell to pieces technically. Roger Penske had two of the best drivers at the time in Al Unser Jr. and Emerson Fittipaldi.

The Penske-built chassis were just not fast enough to qualify on the first weekend. Every day of the following week, Fittipaldi ran as much mileage as possible and still could not coax competitive speed from the Penske chassis. In desperation, Penske bought a Reynard from Pagan Racing. Pagan Racing had set the car up to be more than capable of a good qualifying speed with Roberto Guerrero at the wheel. Pagan literally wheeled the car from its garage to Penske's, and Team Penske "improved" the car by putting its setup on it.

The car never went as fast again. No matter how they tried, Team Penske's engineers could not get enough speed. To the great embarrassment of Roger Penske, Unser, and Fittipaldi, the most successful team in the history of the Speedway failed to get a single car into the race. This is a classic example of the disruptive combination of too much information, too many engineers, not enough clear direction, and probably a little panic. Although this type of situation does not happen often, it does happen from time to time, even to the best teams in the business.

THE RIGHT WAY

Rick Mears is famous for his methodical approach to races like the Indianapolis 500. Mears has always said that he runs the first 450 miles just to be in a position to run fast and at the front for the last 50 miles. During those 450 miles, Mears is constantly feeling what the car does and, more importantly, what the car needs on that particular day and in that particular environment. Over the radio, he will give direction to his crew on what he wants changed during the next pit stop. Sometimes he might know what to change; he will, as accurately as possible, describe the car's symptoms, and he will have his engineer join in the decision-making.

During a race, the engineer is totally powerless to help unless the driver feeds him accurate information. If the driver fails to read the requirements properly and the wrong change is made, the car goes slower. This does happen, but the great champions who have a good technical foundation make more good decisions than bad on average, and this keeps them toward the front of the races more often than not.

Rick Mears was well known for consistently having the right setup changes made to his cars, hence his place in history as a four-time winner of the greatest racing spectacle in the world.

Mario Andretti was a great technical driver. There are some who believe that his career was prolonged because he was so good technically. He could engineer the car to be faster than most, and therefore the bravery of the younger generation was beaten by the engineering genius of experience. There is no doubt that when Andretti won the Formula One world championship, he was in a car that was faster than everything else on the grid. The accurate feedback he provided his engineers was a large part of the reason why the car was faster. Whether Mario was in a Formula One car, an Indy car, a sports car, or a stock car, he could win. This success trait is a hallmark of a good technical driver.

Even rookie Formula One drivers can quickly become known as good technical drivers. Poland's Robert Kubica was credited by BMW for his technical insight and mistake-free pace as major elements that enabled them to develop the BMW car in 2006. Williams Technical Director Sam Michael was instantly impressed by rookie Formula One driver Nico Rosberg. Nico's dad, Keke Rosberg, who was my teammate at Williams in 1982 when he won the world championship, was not a good technical driver—he was pure instinct-reflex. Nico seems to have a different R-DNA makeup because he has developed in a different way from his dad. After Nico Rosberg had been in Formula One for only a short time, Sam Michael said this about him: "I think he can de-brief like an engineer . . . . I have not yet worked with a driver able to give detailed analytical feedback as well as Nico."

The other end of the scale for a Formula One driver might be former Ferrari driver (and Grand Prix winner) Jean Alesi. Alesi was a complete instinct-reflex driver with very little technical knowledge. His lack of technical understanding limited his success in Formula One.

On the track, Alesi was all entertainment. He could drive a car on the edge of adhesion and almost dare it to fly off the road. He could mesmerize a crowd with his performance. There was a downside to his personal pyramid—a lack of understanding of what was going on with the car. His engineers grew frustrated as they were left without accurate technical feedback. AMG Technical Director Gerhard Ungar once issued an ultimatum to his Mercedes DTM team at the end of 2005: "He goes, or I do." That edict led to Alesi being demoted to an old spec car. This lack of technical understanding was also the reason why, despite his brilliant raw speed, Alesi did not enjoy much success in Formula One.

What would you like an engineer to say about you someday? What choices do you have to make in order to make this possible? Are you willing to make those choices? Are you willing to make the necessary sacrifices? How committed are you to being the best you can be?

TECHNICAL SAVVY IS NOT A BORN-WITH TRAIT

None of us were born as good technically sensitive drivers with naturally good feedback; this is a learned trait. Some learn it quickly; some never learn it. Being a good technically sensitive driver requires a considerable amount of discipline because going fast is a driver's natural instinct. A different mindset is required to put aside your desire to go fast and instead drive just below the limit with enough mental capacity resources left to feel the car.

If, as a driver, you tend to be driven by what the stopwatch says and not by feel, I urge you to stop right now and consider how much better you would be if you had more discipline, and if you worked more diligently on a better setup. A racing car that can go faster will always provide you with an advantage. If you start every race with an advantage, you will win more races.

Great technically sensitive drivers of the past include Mario Andretti, Jack Brabham, Mark Donohue, Dan Gurney, Alain Prost, Michael Schumacher, and Jackie Stewart. Current-day technically sensitive drivers include Fernando Alonso, David Coulthard, Gil de Ferran, Jeff Gordon, Robert Kubica, Alex Wurz, Scott Dixon, and Alex Zanardi.

HONESTY

Always be brutally honest with the team. I can't stress this enough. If you can't feel a change, then say you can't feel it. Just because they made a change does not mean you will feel it. The worst thing a driver can do is start spewing technical information, fueled by a desire to sound knowledgeable or by what the stopwatch just indicated. This habit will not allow you to overcome your weakness, and it will not endear you to the team. Honesty always has been and always will be one of the most endearing qualities in anyone.

Motorsports has a habit of flushing everything out of everybody. It is such a challenging sport, physically, mentally, and emotionally, that the truth comes out. Never try to stand on a shaky platform, never try to be what you are not. It will become stamped in your R-DNA, and every team manager will know about it eventually, because they all talk.

ENVIRONMENTAL BENEFITS

Jimmy Vasser once told me that he might not be the best driver in the world, but he was "pretty damn good." I have always admired him because he enjoyed racing so much. Vasser was not regarded as a great technical driver. He could drive a car very fast when it was well set up, but he was not able to consistently steer a team in the right direction technically, and that is why his results were so up and down. He was always at his best when paired with a teammate who could steer the team technically, like Zanardi. Vasser's greatest strength was his mental toughness.

When Mo Nunn was an engineer for Chip Ganassi Racing, mainly concentrating on Zanardi's car, Ganassi asked him to go testing with Vasser at Portland. As a former driver, Nunn has a good idea how drivers work, and he can read how to best handle a situation. During the Portland test, he controlled Vasser's input by only allowing him to do a maximum of three laps at a time. If there were areas of uncertainty, Nunn would backtrack with the technical setup of the car to get back to a known-quantity baseline.

Controlling the test like this did not allow Vasser to get sidetracked or to be tempted to use the stopwatch as a guide to his decision-making. At the end of the test, Vasser had driven faster than anyone had ever gone at Portland. This is an example of a team recognizing how to best manage a situation and creating the right environment within which the driver flourishes. In turn, the team gets quality answers from what is usually an expensive test session.

How many drivers are able to create an environment that allows them personally to flourish? This is not as easy as it sounds because most teams are controlled by managers who don't understand or value the benefits of putting the driver in a beneficial environment. Very few drivers can read their own environment needs accurately, and few have the discipline to slowly try to surround themselves with what they need.

If the driver is honest and open enough to admit to a weakness, that action needs to be supported, and it will go a long way toward creating the necessary environment. A driver's instinct is to go fast. What most of them don't understand is that the speed found in a race car is a byproduct of having everything right.

Tony Kanaan is another very good driver who has shown that his weakness is in the technical department (remember at Indy in 2007, he said that Franchitti was "more picky" than he was). He has great talent and can win races, but without good feel-sensitive teammates, he has not shown the consistent front-running pace of a good technical driver. If Kanaan (or his manager/coach) had recognized this weakness early in his career and worked harder to turn the weakness into a strength, he would be a much more complete driver today. Kanaan has many great strengths, one being his sheer speed in a race car, as long as that car is set up to go fast enough. Another is his ability to mentally process what happens in a race environment. And perhaps Kanaan's greatest attribute is his desire and commitment to the sport.

If you contrast Kanaan with Cristiano da Matta, you will see that they came up through very similar paths. Their Brazilian backgrounds led to a similar karting training ground, then through lower single-seater formulae, then to the CART Indy Lights series in America, where they both won the championship. Within a few years of one another, they both became CART Champ Car drivers.

However, when near the top of the tree and with demands that are much greater, it became apparent that somewhere along the way, da Matta developed a much stronger ability to technically read and adjust a race car. During the CART days when they competed against each other, a pattern developed: da Matta was consistently near the front, and Kanaan was only at the front sporadically.

Some would argue that da Matta might have had a better team. I disagree with this because before da Matta ever drove for Newman/Haas, he was a winner with the much smaller team, PPI, led by Cal Wells. Great drivers have a habit of showing great performances even in smaller teams. Remember Ayrton Senna as a rookie in Formula One, in the wet in Monaco, in a Toleman, where he almost won.

Tony Kanaan went on to win the Indy Racing League (IRL) championship with some stunning performances; however, it is a well-known fact that Tony's teammate, Bryan Herta, was the technical brains behind the team's chassis setup decisions. So the environment that surrounded Kanaan allowed his R-DNA to flourish because his technical weakness was supported from within the team. I believe that Kanaan could have been even more successful over the span of his career *if* he had recognized and overcome his technical weakness much earlier in his career.

Cristiano da Matta's superior technical ability led him to far greater success than Kanaan and ultimately to Formula One. It could be argued that da Matta's technical ability has allowed him to also make millions more dollars for himself and his team. When you get to the top of the tree in motor racing, you simply can't hide a weakness, and the Kanaan/da Matta case is a great example of this.

TECHNICAL R-DNA

Scott Dixon is an example of a very young driver who has achieved significant success. He currently holds the record for the youngest-ever winner of a round of the CART Champ Car series. Dixon is still developing his technical abilities, but even at this stage of his career, his reputation for being good technically is beginning to spread. Chip Ganassi Racing's team manager, Mike Hull, is openly telling people that Dixon knows what the car is doing and, more importantly, knows what he needs it to do to suit him at a particular track. Dixon is able to accurately describe these scenarios, which gives his engineers a solid footing when they tune the car.

Scott Pruett became a good technical driver late in his career. While he was out of Champ Car racing in 1994, Pruett was hired by Patrick Racing to spend a season testing and developing Firestone's new Indy car tires. Pruett did 15,000 miles of testing that year, and he admits that the testing made him a better driver technically. He was forced to become a disciplined test driver because his feedback would determine what tires Firestone would make for the following season.

It's not a coincidence that some of the great champions are also very accurate technical drivers. The 2005 Formula One world champion, Fernando Alonso, is regarded as a driver with a well-developed technical understanding of a race car.

Frenchman Pierre Dupasquier is a legend in Formula One circles. For years, he was Michelin's competition director, and he has worked with some of the sport's greatest drivers. He was an active part of the group that introduced the radial tire to Formula One in the late 1970s with Renault, and since then, his work with Michelin has brought collaborations with many world champions. All of the drivers made a strong impression on him, and Alonso was no different. When it comes to Alonso's work ethic and technical ability, Dupasquier has high praise: "In our job, driver feedback is very important," he said.

"Fernando has always been very precise in his comments. First of all, he has an incredible memory: he can recall the reference numbers of tires used in a test several months previously! He does the first part of the technical analysis for us, making selections. That is a rare quality."

Perhaps the most direct comment about Alonso's technical ability came from Renault Formula One Chief Designer Tim Densham: "From the design side, he's the ideal driver that you want. When you ask him to test something, you want a black and white decision on whether it's better or not. The last thing you want is a driver saying it's better in this corner but maybe not in that one. Fernando is a positive driver in this and has always given us straight answers."

NONTECHNICALLY SENSITIVE R-DNA

One of the more fascinating stars is former Williams/McLaren Formula One driver Juan Montoya. He burst on the Formula One scene after winning the Indy 500 and CART Champ Car championship, and he was initially hailed as the next Michael Schumacher. It was obvious to me that unless Montoya quickly learned more about the technical side of a race car, he would never be as good as Michael Schumacher. Sure, he would win races, but his technical weakness was becoming more apparent each season, and he felt the pressure of a top-line Grand Prix team that needed more technical direction from him.

Juan Montoya's deficiency in the technical department was obvious to the people who knew what to look for, yet Montoya himself denied the suggestion and attempted to place the blame elsewhere for his lack of performance.

"Juan is one of the most talented drivers I have ever seen; his car control is brilliant, and so is his overtaking," enthused former Ferrari driver and manager of the BMW Formula One program, Gerhard Berger. "There is nothing to say about this area; he can do the same as Michael on the driving side. I think it's a question of how he can get the maximum out of his car's setup. That's where he is lacking a bit of experience and has to work harder. It's the only area I can think of where he could improve . . . maybe he can't."

Remember, motor racing flushes out all the strengths and weaknesses.

"You always need to get the maximum out of the car, but what Gerhard has said is completely the opposite to the others who are saying that I'm going too fast with the car and going too hard," said Montoya.

"I think the engineers are going to have to push themselves very hard. It's up to them and us to really go through everything with the car to find its sweet spot.

"I'm happy with the way I'm driving," Montoya continued. "I always try and maximize every lap I do. If I don't know how to maximize the car, then how did I put it on pole position seven times in 2002 when it wasn't 100 percent capable of it?

"Put simply, we were missing a quicker car," said Montoya.

Despite Montoya's obvious annoyance, the bottom line is that when he drove for Williams, neither he nor Ralf Schumacher were technically accurate enough to develop the car, and therefore the team's overall performance suffered. Montoya is a great example of an instinct-reflex driver who can drive the wheels off a car, but you better be able to give him the setup he needs rather than relying upon him to work out what he needs.

His golden opportunity to become a champion came when he was signed by McLaren Mercedes. It is one of the few teams equipped with enough engineering talent on the pit wall to support an instinct-reflex driver like Montoya.

Despite being enamored enough with Montoya to sign him to a contract, McLaren immediately began to recognize his technical weakness and question his level of dedication and commitment. If the high-water mark for a Champion's Pyramid has already been set by Michael Schumacher, you need to at least start at his level to stand a chance of beating him consistently.

When Montoya drove for Chip Ganassi in 1999 and 2000 in the CART championship, he relied totally on brilliant instincts and reflexes (of which he has an abundance). His engineer was Mo Nunn, who had won championships with drivers like Mario Andretti, Emerson Fittipaldi, and Alex Zanardi. Nunn realized very quickly that compared to Zanardi,

Montoya had little knowledge or interest in the technical side of the race car. Montoya's weakness was largely masked by his phenomenal instincts and reflexes as he rose through the lower formulae. He was fast, spectacular, and winning races. However, although he was regarded by some as one of the fastest men in Formula One, his struggles with the Williams BMW team began to highlight his technical weakness. When he was at the top of the tree and racing against some of the world's best drivers, he needed more than just his brilliant instincts and reflexes.

After the 2002 United States Grand Prix, Williams BMW co-owner and Technical Director Patrick Head is on record saying that Montoya needed to up his game if he is to become a champion.

Chief Operations Engineer Sam Michael expands on that: "Both our drivers are certainly capable of being world champions. But they're the same as everyone else in the team in that they need to work harder. It's amazing how much difference a driver can make to the team's motivation—engineers, mechanics, designers, and those at the factory. And maybe that's the difference between our two drivers—and I'm not just pointing the finger here; I think it applies to the rest of the grid too—and the best driver, who is Michael Schumacher.

"You hear stories of Michael phoning up [Ferrari sporting director] Jean Todt at ten o'clock at night and asking about what spring [Luca] Badoer had on this particular lap, as he's been looking at the data, and there was a lap where he was very quick. Our guys just don't do that."

And what do you think the drivers said after comments like these? Ralf Schumacher defended himself: "I find it strange that so many people assume to know exactly how Michael works. I've always thought I had a pretty good insight into that, and I'd be very surprised if Michael would take time away from his family to phone the factory at ten at night. Getting the best out of yourself is not about phoning the factory at night. Besides, if I phoned Williams at that time, there would be no one there."

Montoya had this to say: "I'm tired of hearing all this bullshit about Michael. If we'd had a car as good as his last year, I think we could have won the championship."

What Montoya misses here is that Michael Schumacher had a car as good as it was because his efforts drove the team technically in the right direction, and they therefore built a better car.

In response, Sam Michael says, "Yes, you can say as long as you've got a car with five percent more downforce or twenty more horsepower, you don't need that extra effort. But the game's too tight not to do it now. Everyone is so close. So if a driver goes to make that final bit of effort, like Michael does, it makes a big difference."

In 2004, *Autosport*'s Nigel Roebuck wrote: "For some time now, it has been fashionable in F1 to put Juan Pablo down, to suggest his fitness isn't what it should be, his motivation questionable, his temperament suspect—to intimate, in sum, that the early hype was overblown, that he was never going to be a true superstar of the sport. That said—and without seeking to make excuses for him—I think it's fair to suggest that, during the four seasons in which Montoya has been with Williams, the team has been far less consistently competitive than he anticipated.

"As a racing driver, pure and simple, Montoya reminds me more than anyone of Sweden's Ronnie Peterson, another genius accused of not spending enough time in the gym, of not demonstrating enough commitment to his job. Another, too, who quite possibly relied too much on his talent. Peterson, by his own admission, was clueless when it came to car setup, but so phenomenal was his natural ability, he would drive around a car's shortcomings."

Montoya is a brilliant driver; however, life became more difficult when his competition became Michael Schumacher, Kimi Raikkonen, and Fernando Alonso. To beat these three, you need a driver fully developed in all areas, particularly the technical side. It is apparent that during Montoya's formative years, no series or team taught him the technical side of a race car. This likely happened because his blinding speed kept him winning races. Can you imagine if Montoya (or someone close to him, or a driver coach) had recognized his weakness earlier in his career? If he was a better driver technically, he could drive the Williams team to develop a better car. Armed with a better car, I have no doubt that Montoya would then have a far greater chance of toppling Michael Schumacher or any other driver in the world.

For me, it will be fascinating to watch if Montoya can become a more complete driver. He never did in Formula One and therefore was run out of the competition. American NASCAR racing became his next move, and the same strengths and weaknesses will go along with him. If he does not improve technically, he will end up moving from team to team, struggling to find the type of success that Michael Schumacher and Jeff Gordon have enjoyed.

Being contrasted to Michael Schumacher's work ethic has frustrated many drivers. Consider what one of Schumacher's data engineers, Andrea Stella, said about his work ethic and technical abilities: "Most of our solutions come from discussion within the team, and that is a very enjoyable way of working. Michael has a very good understanding of the car, and this makes our life much easier in a way, because he can give you not only the feeling he has from actually driving the car, but also the feeling on which direction we should go in terms of setting up the car. In fact, I think he could almost engineer his own car!"

That's not to say that a nontechnically sensitive driver such as Montoya cannot become a champion. Keke Rosberg, Mika Hakkinen, and Jimmy Vasser are all examples of nontechnically sensitive drivers who won titles.

So the burning question might be, how can a driver evaluate his skills and determine if he is a good technical driver or not? Put simply, can you feel the suspension and aerodynamic changes (especially the small ones) and determine whether they are the right direction or not? All drivers can feel something in a race car. With something big, like if the car picked up a puncture, most drivers will feel the difference. There are drivers who can feel the basic setup changes, such as spring changes, ride-height changes, and damper changes, etc. Drivers can also tell what the car is doing in certain places on the racetrack. In the lower formulae, this is a lot easier because the speeds are slower, and there is a lot more suspension movement.

The faster the car gets, the stiffer the suspension gets, and the more difficult it becomes to feel the changes. The more technical feel the driver has, the more information he can give the engineers as he drives it fast.

Remember that at the Indianapolis Motor Speedway the changes are becoming so subtle (1/2 degree on just one front wing or 20 thousandths of an inch change on the ride height) that it is almost impossible for the drivers to feel everything, but the great drivers feel the most. The top teams now have decals put on before the final paint clear coat is applied because the edges of the decals cause too much turbulent air at 200 miles per hour. I doubt that a driver can feel this small a change, but the better the technical driver, the smaller the change he can feel.

HOW TO BECOME A BETTER TECHNICAL DRIVER

Going faster is not about driving better, it's about having a better car. Now that you know what you need to do, you must learn how to get it. The key question is: Are you prepared to commit to doing whatever it takes to become a better technical driver? If your answer is a whole-hearted yes, then you have a fighting chance. If this is not a strength of yours, progressing will be hard work. You need to mentally decide whether the end result will be worth it or not. Consider improving your technical abilities as a test of your desire to be the best you can be.

YOUR RESPONSIBILITY

There is no shortcut to learning the technical side of a race car. You cannot learn it from a book, from a video, or from behind a desk. You will only learn it by experiencing it. Make every lap count. Get a note pad, write everything down, and study what it all means. Then get into the habit of taking copies of all setups used on your race car. Get a copy of all software used for the data capture on the race car, and load it onto your computer. Then follow through on your personal commitment and begin to study.

For the instinct-reflex driver, this aspect of the job can be somewhat difficult. In addition to studying and gaining a practical understanding of the technical changes, the driver also has to develop the discipline to drive the car in a more consistent way and not at 10/10ths. It is a very natural thing for an instinct-reflex driver to drive flat out; that's what we love about them. It's also a short-term benefit to the team because the fast laps they turn make the whole team smile. Just remember that every test day spent proving you have great speed (which we already knew) rather than learning how to improve the car is a lost opportunity to further develop the Champion's Pyramid.

THE FORMATIVE YEARS

At as early an age as possible, your mechanic (dad, paid help, friend, whomever) should discuss all technical changes with you prior to changing the car. Whether you are racing a go kart, midget, Formula Ford, or whatever, make it your responsibility to learn what is going on with the car. The glory is in going fast, but there will not be a consistent payback of glory days if you rely on others to create an ideal environment for you. You have a personal responsibility to understand and help control your technical environment.

Make yourself ask questions about the setup. There is no such thing as a stupid question. When changes are made to the car, insist on understanding why and how they affect the car. Never be afraid to ask the mechanics/engineers why or how they made changes. They will be delighted to explain it to you because they know that the better you understand the setup, the more you will help them, and the faster the car will go.

Whenever you go to a test, the team will keep a log of every comment, every lap time, and every change. Make sure you get a copy of this report as soon as you can and study it until you have a very clear picture of what happened and why it happened. If it helps, add your own notes that will help you recall what happened if you need to reference the report at a later time.

When you go home, pull out your setup sheets for the test sessions and go over them lap by lap and change by change. People generally shy away from what they don't know, and it's the same with engineering a car. The more you study and apply yourself to learning about the car, the easier it will be for you to understand the technical side, and the more likely you will be to immerse yourself in it.

How many people do you know who would not buy a computer because they knew nothing about them? After a few months, they are sending emails and surfing the net. Soon, they realize that they can no longer live without it. Learning how to set up a race car is the same. Once you overcome the fear of the unknown, it will pay dividends in results and, in turn, in financial rewards.

STAY ON TRACK

British star Jenson Button learned some lessons the hard way when he raced in Formula One for the first time. He was too casual and did not think enough about what he was doing. He was caught up in the flash and dazzle of F1. He spent more time with his girlfriends than with his engineers. He did realize it, though, before it became too late.

Earlier in the book, I mentioned that relationships and friendships drive motorsports. Team managers and associates talk all the time about drivers and their good and bad points. While a team might not slam a driver, if his weakness is technical, that trait becomes known to everyone. Remember what I said earlier: the truth is the only thing that does not change, and you can't hide the truth for long, hence the need to recognize at an early stage your strengths and weaknesses and make sure you turn any weaknesses into strengths. If you are a good technical driver, that means that any investment in new developments for a car becomes money well spent. Likewise, if a driver gives inaccurate technical feedback, a chunk of the team's budget might easily be wasted. Money spent that doesn't turn into results often leads to finger pointing, which can alienate the driver from the team.

Learning the technical side of racing is not glamorous. A mechanic having to clean up dirty oil from a crashed oil tank is not glamorous either. Remember, the driving force that makes you work through the difficult times is your and your team's vision of capturing a victory due to a job well done.

Bear in mind that drivers have to reach a certain age—usually 14 or older—to be able to really process and understand this type of technical information. This does not mean that you should not bother with it if your child is younger than 14. He still must get into the habit of having the right work ethic, which lays the foundation for him to learn at a much faster rate when he is able to process (and hence retain) the information at a much faster rate in his own brain.

Between ages 14 and 16, the floodgates open with most drivers; they begin to process information a lot faster, and it all begins to make sense. The key to getting those gates to open comes when they learn how to feel the results of changes. When that happens, you have a driver who will have a valuable tool to help himself and his team win.

CHAPTER 4

COMMUNICATIONS

There is no such thing as reality, only perception.

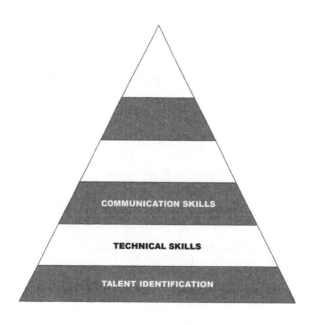

During the Team Green Academy driver-development program in 1996 and 1997, we put many of the drivers through a basic communications course. None of the drivers had ever attended a course like this before, nor had they ever considered attending such a course.

Almost to a man, each young driver said, "If only I had known this information last season." Teams are complex organizations, and communication problems often lead to friction. Knowing how to communicate effectively can relieve those stresses and keep everyone focused on winning races.

Print ads for professional negotiator Chester Karras use the tagline, "You don't get what you deserve, you get what you negotiate." That's as true in racing as it is in life. You get what you negotiate by way of your ability to communicate. You could be the most gifted driver that ever walked the face of the earth, but if you can't use the power of communication to get yourself into the environment that allows you to shine, you won't succeed at the highest levels. You, your friends, and your parents may be the only ones fully aware of your talent.

The dictionary defines communication as the exchange of thoughts, messages, or information by speech, signals, writing, or behavior. You can communicate verbally or with body language. How you position your body is a language all of its own, and it can be an effective way to communicate confidence. Body language can be a hindrance to a driver if it portrays a lack of confidence or a weakness. When someone looks you in the eye during a handshake, there is a connection that can carry sincerity with it. When a driver boldly communicates verbally and with body language, he exudes confidence. Trust can be built quickly with good verbal and body language communication.

The opposite is a driver who looks lost or unsure of himself when meeting someone new. If the handshake is weak, if the eyes wander, and/or if the shoulders are stooped, confidence would not be expressed to the recipient. If the recipient senses that you have a lack of confidence, it becomes harder to prove your worth and value as a driver. Body language has power, and it can be used to open or close doors. People will embrace others they feel they can trust, and trust is built through effective communication.

Something interesting happened when my 15-year-old son, Conor, first met Australian Formula One driver Mark Webber. After the initial handshake, Webber immediately placed his left hand on Conor's lower back and his other hand pushed his upper chest to a more upright position. As he did this, he said to Conor that he should carry himself in a more upright and proud manner because it exudes more confidence. Webber is known for his physical fitness exploits outside the cockpit, and he is a great believer that your physical self is a reflection of your mental and emotional self. He therefore likes to see young drivers exude a confident look and feel that says, "I have the ability and the strengths, and I know where I'm going." Webber even commented on Conor's feet positioning. Conor had a toe-out look, and Webber is a believer that feet pointed straight ahead help the body to be more aligned and therefore to move in the right direction.

Good communication, both verbal and physical, can help create the racing environment that you need to be successful. The opposite is also true, as poor communication is just not as effective. Good communication can be as simple as an email update, a verbal affirmation, a handshake, a nod, or a wink, and most of all, it includes supportive behavior both on and off the track.

SIMPLE EXERCISE

You may be surprised to know that you could give 10 people the same note to read, and all 10 could understand the information differently. If this is possible, then what might happen if the same thing occurred within a team environment, especially when there is so much at stake?

When you work within a team environment, it is possible people can read or see the same information and yet interpret it completely differently. I use a simple exercise to prove this point. Do it *exactly* as I describe below.

Type the following saying 10 times and give it to a group of 10 people. Tell the people that you are simply giving them a card to read and ask them what they think it means.

"Finished files are the result of years of scientific study combined with the experience of many years of experts."

Have everybody read it carefully and try to understand what it means. Ask some of them to explain what they think it means.

Then ask each person to count the number of f's in their sentence (answers will range from three to seven). Ask those that came up with a total less than seven to count how many times "of" appears in the sentence.

Most people come up short because "of" is pronounced "ov" and therefore does not register in the brain as an "f."

The point here is that things are not always what they seem to be. Part of the art of communication is being able to understand what is actually being conveyed, as opposed to what you think or perceive is being communicated.

THERE IS NO SUCH THING AS REALITY, ONLY PERCEPTION

The first time I heard the phrase, "There is no such thing as reality, only perception," I was perplexed. Then I thought hard about it and began to realize it means that what is truth to one is different than what is truth to another. A more accurate use of this phrase might be that there is no such thing as reality, just your perception of reality. Your perception determines your emotional response.

Everybody sees and interprets his reality through his perception. What we term as reality is different for everyone.

Everyone interprets each situation according to how he personally processes information. When you consider how you communicate, you have to allow for the fact that everyone processes information differently, and everyone interprets circumstances differently. It's not unusual for people to start to get a little glassy-eyed when I discuss this subject, but the longer and deeper you think about it, the more you will see what a difference it can make when you communicate effectively with people.

Communication covers a broad spectrum that includes verbal skills, people skills, body language, and situational awareness skills. The first thing any driver needs to fully understand about communication is that motor racing is a team sport. Therefore, you have to communicate, recognize, and appreciate all team members.

I believe the phrase "sticks and stones may break my bones but names will never hurt me" is 100 percent wrong. If you are guilty of verbal abuse of any of your team members, you will live to regret your behavior. Despite the short-term personal satisfaction of blurting out your one-sided story, you will seldom benefit from an emotional outburst.

Communication is your connection to your team. Good communication keeps you plugged into your team and keeps them on your side. You want to be a champion, right? Controlling your emotions is part of the program that will lead to regular appearances on the podium.

TEMPERAMENTS AND PERSONALITIES

Thanks to current behavioral science, we know that people are different from each other in every possible way. They are born with different DNA codes. They have a wide variety of backgrounds, attitudes, and expectations. All of these variables create different styles of communication that are paramount for a driver to understand when dealing with his team and himself. Understanding these differences and likenesses will give a driver an added benefit because so much of his success hinges upon his ability to communicate effectively.

It is common knowledge that there are four primary temperaments (personality types) and, just like blood types, you are born with a certain type. It can never be changed . . . but it can be adjusted.

If you have a basic understanding of the four types of temperaments, you can unlock the door to effective communication. Understanding how a driver's temperament affects his career is another racing skill that will take time to develop and is beyond the grasp of most kids. If the parents understand it, however, they can help young drivers develop and succeed, particularly as the driver progresses to the highest levels of racing and needs to communicate effectively.

Consider this example: What if you are working with what I call a "laptop" race engineer and his communication style requires you to sit down for an hour after each session and accurately discuss, in minute detail, every aspect of the chassis, engine, gearbox, and racetrack? This engineer would probably also want you to pour over data graphs in fine detail in order to provide him with as much information as possible. It is his job then to take all that information, understand it, and use it to help the car go faster. Now, if you simply tell him the car is loose and you're off to play golf, chances are you will not have connected with him, nor will you have satisfied his requirements. This would be an ineffective way to communicate with your engineer.

On the other hand, if your race engineer is what I call a "trench" engineer and all he needs to know are the basics—is the car understeering (pushing) or is it oversteering (loose)—and you want to sit down for an hour with him to explain every aspect in minute detail and ask him to spend hours studying data graphs when that's not how he operates effectively, again you will not have connected with him nor satisfied his requirements.

What if you had the skills to be able to read what type of person you might be dealing with? What if you knew the temperaments of all the people on your team and were able to walk in through their particular doors of communication? That would give you a head start to having effective communication with the people who matter on your team.

What I'm about to tell you is known by every major corporation in the country. Major companies spend vast amounts of money getting their employees to understand the different temperaments of people. In fact, many people are not hired until they have taken a full personality profile (temperament profile) test because the company wants all people to be working in their personal positions of strength. Understanding temperaments helps you work and communicate more effectively.

THE FOUR BASIC TEMPERAMENTS

The Greek names for the four basic primary temperaments (personality types) are Choleric (doer), Sanguine (talker), Phlegmatic (watcher), and Melancholy (thinker). Everyone on a race team will fit into one of these categories, and each individual will be a blend of a dominant personality type and a secondary.

Choleric (doer): These people are results-oriented leaders and managers, and they are very driven. Making friends is not their priority. They would be somewhat traditional, be decisive, and have a touch of prestige about them. You usually find these people in team manager roles.

Sanguine (talker): They are fun at all costs, bright, colorful party people, and generally outgoing and entertaining. They usually have a lot of friends. Life is all about adventure, excitement, and being active. You usually find these outgoing people in public relations, sales, and marketing.

Phlegmatic (watcher): These people are easygoing, are nonoffensive and loyal, and are usually good followers. In other words, they carry out their job lists. They would be somewhat people-centered, romantics, and family-oriented and would enjoy togetherness. These would be mechanics and other race support staff.

Melancholy (thinker): These people are deep thinkers, very black and white, and extremely analytical, and they can often appear to be moody. They can be visionary, perfectionists, and like to plan ahead, and they would be regarded as being competent. These would be race team engineers.

Now let's look at what behaviors each temperament might exhibit.

Always remember that everybody has a blend of dominant and secondary, so your melancholy race engineer could have a sanguine blend, which lightens his persona. Your doer (choleric) team manager could be a fun-loving talker (sanguine) as a secondary, or he could be an extremely analytical thinker (melancholy) as a secondary.

The real key to effective communication is two-fold: how to project your own personality and wishes, and how to recognize the personalities of the people you are dealing with in order to communicate most effectively with them. The following table will give you the clues you need when learning to read what type of personalities you are dealing with.

BEHAVIOR	CHOLERIC (DOER)	SANGUINE (TALKER)	PHLEGMATIC (WATCHER)	MELANCHOLY (THINKER)
PRIMARY CHARACTERISTICS/ STRENGTHS	Go-getters, ambitious	Networkers, socializers	Peacemakers, bridge builders	Fact finders, pragmatists
WHAT THEY TALK ABOUT	I will . . . results; what they want to achieve; talk objectively; avoid small talk	I want. . . what they want, dreams and aspirations; tell stories	I feel. . . share personal feelings	I think. . . numbers, facts; talk objectively; avoid small talk
HOW THEY TALK	State commands, direct assertion	State commands, direct assertion	Inquire, indirect assertion	Inquire, unimposing
TONE OF SPEECH	Louder, use voice to emphasize points	Louder, easily excited; Use voice to emphasize points	Quieter, do not vary voice much	Quieter, do not vary voice much
PACE OF SPEECH	Very fast	Fast	Slower	Moderate
BODY LANGUAGE	Lean forward, limited or no facial expressions, intense eye contact, deliberate movements	Lean forward, controlled facial expressions, good eye contact, lots of gestures	Lean back, some facial expressions, good eye contact, use gestures	Lean back, limited or no facial expressions, limited eye contact, limited gestures
COMMUNICATION STYLE	Direct, to the point, can be outspoken, formal, business-like	Animated, excitable, can come on too strong, informal, casual	Dreamy thoughts, may seem vague, informal, casual	Specific, concise, clear, logical, formal, bottom line

continued from page 123

BEHAVIOR	CHOLERIC (DOER)	SANGUINE (TALKER)	PHLEGMATIC (WATCHER)	MELANCHOLY (THINKER)
RESPONSIVENESS	May appear pushy, more reserved and cautious, can appear preoccupied	Open and warm, animated, enthusiastic, enjoy the conversation	Friendly, responsive, enjoy the conversation	May appear unresponsive, reserved, and cautious; can appear preoccupied
LISTENING PATTERN	Can be poor listeners, want to control conversation, may interrupt, like to summarize	Listen, react to what you are saying, talk a lot	Good listeners, react to what you are saying, caring	Listen but may appear not to
MOTIVATED BY	Results	Applause	Approval	Activity
THRIVE ON	Pressure, change	Stimulation, fun	Togetherness, support	Accuracy, information
EXPRESSION OF ANGER	Impatient, aggressive	Easily frustrated, can be explosive	Gentle, get flustered	Slow to anger, rational approach
WORK STYLE	Work in priority order, make priority lists, do several things at once, intense, driven	Unstructured, like freedom, lots of people interaction, make lists of people to call and places to go	Easygoing, cooperative, always willing to be of service, go with the flow, no strong sense of urgency	Thorough, attentive to detail, step-by-step procedures, work in sequence, to-do lists, one thing at a time, pensive
WORK AREA	Functional, organized, work in priority order	Interesting things, gadgets, novelty items, giveaways always readily displayed	Sentimental mementos and souvenirs, pictures of family and friends, desk may appear cluttered	References are at fingertips, lots of paper, work is in piles

BEHAVIOR	CHOLERIC (DOER)	SANGUINE (TALKER)	PHLEGMATIC (WATCHER)	MELANCHOLY (THINKER)
WORK PACE	Work fast, a whirlwind, like change	Faster, bore easily, move from one thing to another	Slower, rarely in a hurry, need time to change, dislike pressure	Methodical, steady stream of work, like a predictable routine
GROUP ROLE	Leader, need to control	Rapport builder, need to be the center of attention	Peacemaker, need to feel included	Information provider, need focus and direction
WHILE UNDER STRESS	Command	Attack	Give in	Avoid
DISLIKE	Wasting time	Reinventing the wheel	Confrontation	Being wrong
STYLE	Formal, business-like	Informal	Go with the flow	Formal, business-like

Now that you have learned how to read the personalities you are dealing with, the following table will help you understand how to communicate more effectively with them.

WHEN DEALING WITH	You should be brief and effi-cient, get to the bottom line, give them options, let them feel in control. You should not stall or beat around the bush, get too personal.	You should show interest, demonstrate personal involvement, compliment them. You should not get straight down to business, dwell on details, talk down to them.	You should be easy and informal give them time, and be agreeable. You should not hurry or confront them.	You should talk facts, be accurate, tell them exactly what you will do and when. You should not be vague, inconsistent, illogical, or overly casual.
MAKE DECISIONS BASED ON	Reaching goals	Intuition	Feelings	Evidence

continued from page 125

BEHAVIOR	CHOLERIC (DOER)	SANGUINE (TALKER)	PHLEGMATIC (WATCHER)	MELANCHOLY (THINKER)
WAYS TO GROW	Listen more, pressure others less, curb competitive independent spirit, be less impersonal and task oriented, be more patient and tolerant, watch your need to take control, be less condescending, take on less, give yourself longer lead times	Pay more attention to details, avoid coming on too strong, don't intimidate others, get down to business quicker, avoid over-reacting, don't be dramatic, talk less, don't always steal the limelight, state your case objectively, don't dominate conversation	Watch your pace, avoid being too slow, initiate and take action, set deadlines, be more assertive, don't get too personally involved, organize your thoughts, don't get flustered under pressure	Reduce your concern for facts and figures, trust your intuition, be more flexible and less of a perfectionist, don't be judgmental, develop relationships, avoid too much detail, make decisions quicker, be more spontaneous, give more praise, avoid being aloof
GOALS	Set many goals, reach your goals by focusing on the results	Goals kill spontaneity, reach your goals by telling others	Cautious about commitment, achieve goals with someone else	Goals must be met on time, be flexible about your deadlines
WANT TO BE APPRECIATED FOR	Productivity and making an impact	For contribution and giving others opportunities	Involvement and being considerate of others	Quality and sound judgment
LIKE TO GET REWARDED WITH	Power	Recognition	Approval	Responsibility
HOW THEY ARE STROKED	Give more responsibility, hold to high expectations	Tell others about them, ask their opinion, give lots of praise	Say thank you, send cards, flowers, or gifts, make them feel special	Value their judgment, give them more autonomy

So now let's deal with you. Which category do you fit in? What type of temperament/personality would be your dominant and what would be your secondary trait? Bear in mind, a personality trait is like your blood type—you have it for life, and you can't change it. What you can change, however, is how you present your temperament/personality to others. If you would like to assess your own personality, go to www.discprofile.com.

Over the years, I have had to temper my aggressive and sometimes abrupt style because it very often does not lay a good foundation for constructive communication. My one-track mind during my early career right up through Formula One was not conducive to professional relationships that would have greatly helped me at the time. Why was I like this, you might ask? Because I knew no other way. I was not fortunate enough to have anyone teach me the basic facts of communication. When I look back at my early years in Formula One, I see a driver (me) who not only drove with an instinct-reflex mentality, but who also lived his life in a similar fashion. Decisions were made without much thought, and it often led to a shoot-from-the-hip mentality. I believe this behavior contributed slowly to ending my Formula One career.

Many people would like to be a sanguine because they love life and people love them. Bear in mind that the sanguine's fun-at-all-costs attitude sometimes makes it difficult for to convince team managers that he is serious about his craft. Examples of racers who are sanguines (talkers) are Jean

Alesi, Gerhard Berger, Helio Castroneves, Tony Kanaan, and Kenny Wallace.

Dario Franchitti is probably a melancholy/phlegmatic (thinker/watcher) blend. His melancholy side shows in his desire for neatness and particular tastes in his car and driving gear—his seat has to fit perfectly, and he is very particular with items like the fit and finish of his driving suit. His easygoing style is a typical phlegmatic trait. You can see that Franchitti's dominant side is melancholy, as he does not like dramatic change and likes to talk facts. He needs an engineer who is a straight shooter and who is emotionally supportive.

Nigel Mansell is a good example of a choleric/melancholy (doer/thinker). He is definitely not a sanguine or phlegmatic. He is aggressive and in your face. With Mansell, it is his way or the highway. Mansell does not make a lot of friends, and an astute team manager would have realized that Mansell needs a strong-minded engineer who is not easily intimidated. If Mansell respects you, he will follow you. Mansell does not need any emotional support from the team to perform well. In fact, he thrives in hostile environments and revels in proving how good he is. The best way to communicate with Mansell is to be direct, clear, and not too personal (he doesn't like fluff).

One of the great American superstars, A.J. Foyt, was a choleric dominant (doer) who did a lot for the sport with a swashbuckling style. Foyt was like Mansell. All through his career, people knew that it was Foyt's way or the highway. Even when he retired and ran his own teams, he still insisted on doing things his way. Unfortunately, his way was the old way, and the modern world had moved on without him. The modern way is the only way to be successful now.

Foyt was successful in an era when close enough was good enough. If a driver complained about a handling issue, he would be told to keep his foot on the power longer. That era is no more because the modern era is so much more specialized. Drivers in the past were the engineers and mechanics. Foyt was a control freak (choleric trait) who dominated every area of the team. He's still a control freak, but today there has to be room for laptops, setup sheets, and de-brief sessions. Working in that kind of excruciating detail goes against the grain of Foyt's personality. The more specialized the modern race teams became, the further from the front of the grid Foyt's cars were.

Jimmy Vasser is a phlegmatic (watcher). He is easygoing, does not rock the boat, and will not cause trouble in the team. His engineer needs to be strong-willed to make sure he steers Vasser the right way. To communicate effectively with Vasser, an engineer needs to understand that he will not work well sitting in front of data charts for half the night. He is relationship-driven and likes to get personal.

Sam Hornish is also in the phlegmatic (watcher) category. Hornish is supremely gifted as a driver, but outside the cockpit his world moves a lot slower than most. He does not rock the boat, he is very compliant to the wishes of others, and he will go with the flow. To manage Hornish effectively, don't put unnecessary pressure on him and keep things as organized as possible.

How do you treat your family, your friends, your coworkers, and/or your race team members? How you treat them could determine how they treat you.

Jeff Gordon is a good communicator. Whether this is a natural trait or a learned one, I don't know. What I do know is that Jeff's ability to communicate and energize people is part of what has made him so successful for so long.

In 1998, NASCAR's most prolific and successful team—Jeff Gordon and his crew chief Ray Evernham—was split up when Evernham left Hendrick Motorsports to form his own team. Gordon and Evernham had won three Winston Cup Championships together. Shortly after Evernham's departure, Gordon's over-the-wall pit crew, known as the Rainbow Warriors, also left. This much change is usually a devastating blow to drivers and teams.

At that time, Jeff Gordon could have easily become dejected and left the ship rudderless. Instead, he got behind his new team and, over the course of the following years, helped guide and lead them to winning his fourth Winston Cup Championship in 2001 with a new group of committed people. He did this through total support, which was demonstrated to them through good communication and supportive behavior. It is no coincidence that every time Jeff

Gordon is in the victory circle the first thing he says is, "Thank you to my team."

In the 2002 Indianapolis 500, Gil de Ferran left the pit lane toward the end of the race and a rear wheel fell off. This undoubtedly cost de Ferran a win at the biggest racing event in the world. Just think what would have happened if de Ferran had elected to vent his anger and verbally abuse his team for the mistake. I doubt he would have had much support for the rest of the season. Instead, he went to each team member, shook their hands, and said thank you for their personal efforts and commitment. De Ferran knows that for the long-term success of his team, and therefore himself, he must always understand that people make mistakes and that success only comes for a driver with the coordinated efforts of a team of people. The following year, the same team, which respected and supported its driver, worked flawlessly, and Gil de Ferran finally won the world's biggest motorsports event, the Indianapolis 500.

Three-time Formula One world champion Ayrton Senna was a great communicator, and his most effective way of communicating with his team was through touch and verbal affirmation. Every morning upon arrival at the racetrack, he would personally shake hands with each of his mechanics, and every evening before he left, he would do the same thing. It was his simple and effective way of saying thank you. Every mechanic loved to get the handshake because to them it was an affirmation of friendship and of respect for what they were doing.

In 1993, I covered Formula One for ESPN, and at the opening race of the season in South Africa, I found myself standing outside the McLaren pit waiting to do an interview with Michael Andretti. When Andretti's teammate, Ayrton Senna, walked through the back door, he recognized me and walked around both of the race cars, zigzagged past half a dozen mechanics, and came straight over to me with his hand outstretched to introduce himself. I had never met Senna before, but like everyone else in motorsports, I had admired him. He had become familiar with me through his knowledge of the history of Formula One and through his interest in following Indy car racing on television, where I was the commentator.

I was completely floored that a multiple-time world champion, who usually has to hide from fans and admirers, would take the time to introduce himself. That simple gesture of communication had a profound effect on me.

My basic understanding of temperaments has revolutionized my relationships and attitudes toward drivers and even my own son, Conor. Conor is a phlegmatic (watcher) just like my younger brother was. My dad misread my brother's behavior as being lazy.

Because I was choleric/melancholy (worker), my brother was always compared to me, and he therefore suffered the well-meaning wrath of my dad. My dad thought he could force my brother into becoming a choleric (doer).

It is a bit like trying to force him to have a different blood type. My brother eventually worked out for himself what he needed to do to become successful. He raced against Ayrton Senna in the karting world championships in Portugal and became a multiple motorsports champion in Ireland. It was very easy for my dad (as it is for many parents) to misread a phlegmatic in this way because he is a watcher and not a doer.

A phlegmatic's gift is that he is a watcher.

In Conor's early career development (12–15 years old), I would push him to download his data from the kart's onboard computer, fill out the lap charts with all relevant information, and work on the kart more. Because he was not wired to be a worker (choleric or melancholy), it was not natural for him to do things like I was asking. It started to build up resentment between us, and we would have heated discussions about it.

Now parents and coaches all around me might think, ah, but he has to learn those things. Yes, he does, but at 12–15 years old, it was not his time.

So instead of race weekends being a time where he felt he was being judged and/or threatened by trying to force him to do unnatural-for-a-phlegmatic things, the weekends became more relaxed and our relationship started to grow. On the racetrack, he responded by driving with an ease that allowed him to display all of his talents (and usually put him at or very close to the front).

A PERSONAL BLUNDER

In 1981, at the British Grand Prix in Silverstone, England, I was driving the March Formula One car in front of many of my family and friends. I always regarded the British Grand Prix as my home race. It was a very emotional event for me and a very important race for me to perform well in. It was an unusual year in Formula One because of the legal cheating that went on with artificially raised ride heights in the pit lane. Essentially, each car had to have a certain ride height when measured in the pit lane. That same ride height was supposed to be maintained out on the circuit, but most teams had hydraulic lowering devices fitted to the shock absorber and spring platforms that would allow the car to run lower to the ground. This allowed the underbody (which generated most of the downforce) to run closer to the ground, which generated more downforce and therefore the car went much faster. My team did not have this lowering device for the first six races, and I failed to even qualify for a starting position. I had one of Ireland's best-known companies, Guinness, as my primary sponsor for the 1981 season, so there was a huge emotional investment in the British Grand Prix, and I was hoping, deep within my heart, for a good showing.

My chief mechanic, Ray Boulter, was a dedicated worker with a wonderful London cockney accent. He was just as frustrated as I was that we had failed to qualify in the first six races of the season. Before the first practice session as we talked loosely in the garages, Boulter was having some good, light-hearted fun at my expense, saying that Grand Prix drivers don't know what hard work is and most spend their time relaxing in armchairs. Everybody laughed at the time, but for some reason, I did not let it roll off me as I should have.

I had a pretty good qualifying session, and the Irish hospitality was in full force in the paddock. I spent the night before the race with family and friends, and there was an air of great anticipation when we talked about whether or not it "might be" the race.

Race day dawned, and the buildup only heightened everybody's anticipation of what might come as the afternoon unfolded. I felt good. The car was giving me the right feelings. I had an unusual confidence in the car that day, and I eagerly awaited the start.

The start of a Formula One race is without a doubt the most dangerous time in motorsports. When the green flag flies, the cars all scream away from a standstill with drivers fighting to get the best traction from the rear tires. The adrenaline rush provided by the run to the first corner usually has drivers' heart rates above 185 beats per minute.

On the first lap of the race, my gearshift came loose and I could not change gears. I had to make an immediate pit stop. The opportunity for glory (a relative term) had disappeared. The machine had broken, and so had the hearts of my family and supporters. I was absolutely livid that all the efforts to try to gain a good result had just been thrown away. Boulter had made a small mistake and forgotten to tighten up the retaining nut on the gear shift after it was adjusted in the cockpit just before the start of the race. By the time he grabbed his wrench and tightened it, I was already in last place and more than half a lap behind.

Almost unbelievably, when I did start to lap at full speed, the car was really fast. I began to catch and pass many cars. Although my efforts were somewhat futile, I still felt compelled to prove a point. Although the race was almost two hours long, it seemed to go by in a flash. The last car I passed before the checkered flag was Frenchman Jacques Lafitte's Ligier, which actually finished on the rostrum in third place. It was one of those days when I was on top of my form and the car was very good, and as I closed in on Lafitte I could still feel my anger because I knew I had missed out on a possible rostrum position in my home Grand Prix. What a day that would have been for me, my friends, and my family.

At the end of the race, as I walked down the pit road with helmet in hand, I saw Boulter walking toward me to offer his congratulations for a job well done. As we approached each other in the pit lane, I was seconds from exhibiting the very poor communication skills that I possessed. The first thing that blurted out of my mouth was, "Remember that armchair you mentioned yesterday—well, you must have been sitting in it."

Boulter's face changed immediately. He didn't know whether to respond verbally or physically. A caustic cloud descended over the team. My team manager, John MacDonald, sided with Boulter and warned me against attacking his employees.

I slowly began to realize that the short-term satisfaction gained by blasting Boulter might not have been a very professional way to handle things. Little did I know what I did for the morale of the team. I learned in the coming weeks that my unwarranted blurt of anger had broken the bond between driver and team. My short-term satisfaction had long-term implications. For the rest of the season, we just went through the motions. Boulter felt betrayed and indeed abused. If only someone had told me about the art of communication, I could have handled the situation entirely differently, and I would have benefited in the long term from a closely knit team.

Twenty-five years later, I still remember that outburst, and I'm fairly sure that Ray Boulter also remembers it. I destroyed the vital foundation necessary for harmony within a team, and make no mistake about it, harmony brings speed. Just imagine what might have happened if I had offered my hand to Ray and thanked him for his countless hours of toil and effort and told him not to worry about the small mistake. What if I also offered that "We win together and we lose together"? I dare say he would have been energized to provide me with the best possible car he could for the rest of the season.

A CHAMPION'S WAY TO COMMUNICATE

Michael Schumacher is a wonderful communicator. He is not necessarily a warm personality, but his enormous success endears him to his hard-working teammates. He is particularly gifted at communicating with his engineers about what he needs in the racing car to make him go faster. History has shown that he is usually right in the direction he sends the team.

His thank-you language is in the form of gifts for his mechanics. Regularly, he presents his mechanics and their families with gifts. He commands a certain respect, and his on-track performances energize the teams he is involved with. A great example of this is when Schumacher drove for the Benetton team between 1992 and 1995. He raised the level of that team to the point that he won two world championships with them. At that same time, the Ferrari team couldn't get out of its own way. When Schumacher left Benetton, the team immediately fell to pieces, and when he joined Ferrari, he helped build that team to be the best in the world. If Schumacher was not such an effective a communicator, I dare say that the Ferrari team would not have been as successful.

As you ponder what type of personality you have and how you believe you interact with other people, I would give a guideline: rather than look to build friendships with people, look to build respect. Respecting others is a great foundation for them to respect you. Respect, in turn, builds your friendships, and friends help friends.

CHAPTER 5

MENTAL SKILLS

Never allow circumstances to dictate your behavior.

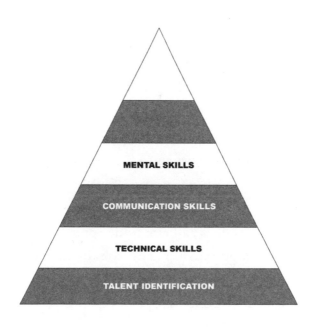

Some people would argue that strong mental skills might be the most critical part of a race car driver's overall package. Without complete emotional and mental control, it is doubtful you can consistently withstand the enormous pressure at the top of the motorsports mountain, and consequently you cannot consistently produce your peak performance.

Mental toughness is easy to measure. You can get an indication as to the mental makeup of a person at a very early age. By four or five years old, children who display a strong sense of individualism and independent thinking usually carry those traits throughout their lives. Children who are emotionally fragile early in their lives can also carry that trait into adulthood.

The world-class athletes who have long careers usually possess great mental strength. Harry Brauvert once wrote in *USA Today* that Tiger Woods' biggest club is his mental strength. He wrote that, "[Tiger's] will to win, combined with his physical conditioning, is unrivaled on PGA Tour. For all the physical skills the golf gods gave Tiger Woods, the mental toughness he brings to his sport might be just as important in setting him apart. A fiery competitor who often pumps his fist to punctuate clutch shots, Woods can focus to the exclusion of all else under pressure, especially when a major championship is on the line. He won eight majors, and he was only twenty-eight."

Pro golfer Bob May once said of Woods, "You can never get

him down, and he will never let himself get down. That's where he really beats up on people. His mental game is every bit as good as his physical game. If he's seven shots out, he still thinks he can win."

Mark O'Meara, probably Woods' closest friend on the PGA Tour, says Woods has a single-minded mental toughness that drives him to be the best at whatever he does.

I believe that there are racing drivers with this same mindset. Bear in mind that a mistake may cost Tiger Woods, at worst, a lost ball; a race car driver could pay for a mistake with his life.

If I look back at my biggest weakness while I competed in Formula One and Indy cars, it was that I was not as mentally strong as I needed to be to sustain great performances. I made too many mistakes under pressure. This led to me throwing away good results in the closing stages of races.

In 1978, at the Austrian Grand Prix, I was presented with an ideal opportunity to shine. It was raining on race day, and rain can be a great equalizer. I reveled in the conditions throughout the race and, in the closing stages, brought the low-budget Ensign in to fourth place. As the racing line dried, it became more critical where I placed the car on the road. With 11 laps to go, I made a small mistake and threw the race away with a spin into a wheat field. In one split-second loss of focus, all the hours of effort by my mechanics and all the hopes and dreams of the team slid off the road. My first world championship points were thrown away, and therefore the valuable financial aid the team (from FOCA, Formula One Constructors Association) would have received the following year also disappeared. If only I had maintained my concentration and focus a little longer.

In 1982, while driving for the Williams Grand Prix team at the Belgian Grand Prix in Zolder, I was running in fifth place when Eddie Cheever began to catch me in the Ligier. Instead of concentrating on my own race, I began to get distracted by Cheever, and I braked a few feet too late into the first corner.

The car locked its rear brakes, and I slid off the circuit backward into the fence. Again, I had exhibited poor mental skills.

In 1983, while driving Indy cars for Tony Bettenhausen at Road America, I was running in third position with a handful of laps to go when I made a small mistake going through the 160-mile-per-hour kink. I slipped off the road and crashed.

These three incidents highlight how I practiced the genesis of self-sabotage. The lesson to take from this is to be honest about your own skills.

If I had been more aware of the problem, I may have been able to find ways to improve. Admitting a weakness is 90 percent of curing it if you are committed to being the very best you can be.

Derek Daly began his career as a race car driver in a 1952 Ford Anglia E93A. This photograph was taken in 1969, when he was 16 years old. *Derek Daly collection*

Daly won two championships in a Mini and is shown here in 1969. *Derek Daly collection*

Formula Ford in England was cutthroat in 1976. Daly won 23 races in a Hawke DL15/17. *Derek Daly collection*

Derek Daly and his mentor Derek "Big D" McMahon during the 1977 Formula 3 season. *Derek Daly collection*

Mo Nunn advises Derek Daly (in the Ensign Formula 1 car) during the 1978 Formula 1 season. *Derek Daly collection*

Derek Daly drove for Williams in 1982 and almost won the Grand Prix of Monaco. *Derek Daly collection*

The last time Daly competed in Daytona (1992), he put a Nissan on the pole. *Derek Daly collection*

Daly and Mario Andretti share a light-hearted moment. *Derek Daly collection*

Daly interviews Jackie Stewart on the grid at the U.S. Grand Prix. Jackie was one of the first drivers to understand that a driver needs a complete package of skills in order to succeed. *Derek Daly collection*

Daly interviews Gil de Ferran in Indianapolis. Gil was a great "feel-sensitive" driver who understood how to communicate well with people. *Derek Daly collection*

Instead of working out, 1982 world champion Keke Rosberg made helmet tie straps that he attached to the sides of the cockpit to support his head. *LAT*

Ayrton Senna had the complete package, and he was driven to be the best. *LAT*

Ayrton Senna had an ability to focus intensely on his job. *LAT*

Ayrton Senna scored an emotional Grand Prix win in Brazil in 1993. *LAT*

Part of Ayrton Senna's communication style was to shake hands with each of his mechanics each day; they loved it. *LAT*

Alain Prost's prepraration was meticulous, and many believe this gave him an edge. *LAT*

Prost was another deep thinker who could strategically plan a race and then execute the plan. *LAT*

Part of Prost's greatness was his ability to be mechanically sympathetic with the car. He won his fourth world championship in a superior car that he helped develop. *LAT*

Rick Mears won the Indy 500 four times because he was a good feel-sensitive driver and had good mental skills. *Dan Boyd*

Mario Andretti put a lot of thought into the setup of his cars. *Dan Boyd*

Mario Andretti was viewed as a fierce competitor who would make life as difficult as possible for everyone he raced against. *Dan Boyd*

Nigel Mansell had great mental skills and loved to prove the doubters wrong by winning. *LAT*

Nigel Mansell—shown in Hungary in 1986—drained himself physically and emotionally in a race car. *LAT*

Dale Earnhardt Sr. was a true champion who understood what it took to dominate on the racetrack. *Nigel Kinrade*

Al Unser Jr. was very disciplined in a race car. *Don Boyd*

Michael Andretti grew to be one of the very best. *Paul Webb*

The McLaren team determined that Michael Andretti had not made a total commitment. *LAT*

Daly (and others) believe that Michael Schumacher had the strongest desire and commitment of any modern driver. Prior to Ferrari, Schumacher raced on the Benetton team. *LAT*

Michael Schumacher's commitment to win led him to literally assault drivers with his car, as when he hit Jacques Villeneuve in Jercz in 1997. *LAT*

Michael Schumacher in the familiar red Ferrari—one of the fastest cars on the grid because of his technical input to the engineers. *LAT*

Michael Schumacher had a thorough understanding of the technical side of race cars and had the ability to pull out the magic lap when needed, particularly in Monaco, a race he won five times. *LAT*

Michael Schumacher shares a moment with chief mechanic Nigel Stephne. *LAT*

Paul Tracy wins in Milwaukee in the Lola that allowed him to enter corners faster because of a more responsive front end. *Paul Webb*

Jean Alesi won for Ferrari in Canada in 1995, but he never became a champion because he lacked the technical skills to understand how to set up a car effectively. *LAT*

Heinz-Harald Frentzen did not perform at the highest levels while at Williams because his mental skills were not at a high enough level. *LAT*

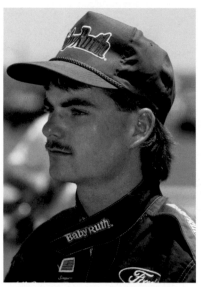

When Daly first met Jeff Gordon, Gordon had the look and feel of a racer who was driven to be the very best. *Nigel Kinrade*

Jeff Gordon wins his first championship. *Nigel Kinrade*

Jeff Gordon has proven that he can sustain high performance through car and team personnel changes. *Nigel Kinrade*

Jeff Gordon proved he was a great leader by winning more championships after he lost crew chief Ray Evernham and the Rainbow Warriors pit crew. *Nigel Kinrade*

The great Penske team experienced technical turmoil in 1995. *Dan Boyd*

Jimmy Vasser excelled when surrounded by the right type of team. *Paul Webb*

Alex Zanardi has proven many times that he has the desire and commitment needed to succeed at the highest levels. *Paul Webb*

When Zanardi won at Laguna Seca, California, in 1998, he displayed all his brilliance—the ability to develop a fast setup and the ability to become an instinct-reflex driver when needed. *Paul Webb*

Frank Williams did not believe that Jenson Button had enough experience to lead his team. *LAT*

Kimi Raikkonen's mental skills are so strong that his first Grand Prix win, in Malaysia in 2003, hardly raised his emotional state. *LAT*

Juan Montoya is one of the most gifted drivers ever. His weakness is on the technical side, and that is why he ended up racing stock cars. *Nigel Kinrade*

Fernando Alonso celebrates winning his first world championship. *LAT*

OTHER STARS

In January 2000, *Autosport* magazine wrote this about a new star on the Formula One horizon, England's Jenson Button.

"Today Jenson Button has the quality and the talent to do the job in F1 and be a great driver. The problem now is that the road is still very long until he is in a position to win the world championship. What will make the difference will be his determination and motivation at the highest level. F1 is very difficult for a young person—the money, the business, the people, everything. You cannot say he is going to be a future world champion or not. That depends on his head."

I always find it fascinating to compare the mental makeup of great drivers. Kimi Raikkonen and Juan Montoya are regularly compared. In November 2004, Nigel Roebuck made an accurate comparison of the two:

"Raikkonen rarely betrays more than a withering glance of emotion, doesn't let in anything that's not relevant to the job in hand. Montoya, fiery and extroverted, wears his heart on his sleeve, and the styles of their racing reflect these traits. Kimi's performances are relentless; Juan Pablo's are a heady mix of adrenaline and opportunism. Raikkonen retains his icy calm every second he's in the car; Montoya uses emotion to drive his performances. Each trait has its up and down sides.

"Raikkonen has the dimmer switch on the outside world turned way down, and there are no distractions.

"Raikkonen's personality lends itself better to focus;

Montoya's is perfect for the element of ambush that wins him races.

"Both drivers are generally immune to pressure from behind, more so than Michael Schumacher. No quarter is given though each is scrupulously fair in battle, with very fine judgment.

"Montoya will be good at the well-timed wind-up just as Kimi will be good in not even acknowledging it.

"The team can perhaps help him in finding more consistent technical solutions than he was able to do at Williams.

"Kimi is just as fast, more flexible, calmer, and already has the momentum of a good team relationship. Nothing is going to faze him, not even a sister silver car going 'round his outside in a place he'd never even considered."

Make no mistake about it: both Montoya and Raikkonen have exhibited these same mental and emotional traits since they were small boys.

MENTAL SKILLS

Mental Pressure: Do You Feel It or Apply It?

Motor racing makes very high demands on us mentally. We are expected to perform in a dangerous sport under enormous pressure with the eyes of the world firmly focused on us. No matter how critical of us our peers are or how caustic the media is, you must not let your guard down for several reasons. First, mistakes can kill you in a race car, and second, at all times, there will be any number of drivers ready and waiting to step into your seat at the slightest opportunity. What other sport do you know where a driver can be killed and there would be a line of willing drivers ready to step into his seat? Motorsport is a colorful, glamorous, savage sport that can be so brutal. It is your job to always rise above this.

There will always be pressure when competing at a world-class level in anything, but if you allow the pressure to disrupt your routine and decision making, you are a driver that feels the pressure. If you use these situations to your advantage and to destabilize your opposition, you are a driver that applies pressure. Try to make sure you are the applier.

Every young driver has a unique mental makeup. While it is a given that everyone needs emotional support of some sort, some drivers require vastly different types of support.

If we talk mental strength, we are talking about what takes place in the head. Whenever there is talk of what goes on inside the head, I have found that most young drivers run for cover. That's because most young drivers will try to hide a weakness, particularly if it has to do with the head. The head is also one of the most complex areas to work with. There is no doubt that working with any world-class athlete can be a real challenge.

Some have theorized that race car drivers are a bit on the disturbed side. In the December 2003 issue of *Formula 1* magazine, Gerald Donaldson wrote:

"Formula One drivers have long captured the imagination

of those who specialize in studying human behavior. Among the first to investigate their psyches were certain disciples of Sigmund Freud [who theorized that] racing was a dangerously deviated carnal game.

"Melanie Klein psychoanalyzed several drivers and decided they were deeply disturbed little boys. According to Klein, cornering a racing car represented coitus with mother, and the threat of an accident was symbolic of 'castration from dangerous paternal phallic symbols.' Klein and company capped off the Freudian fantasies by equating the traditional spraying of champagne by the drivers on the podium with male orgasm and ejaculation. And Peter Fuller concluded that motor racing is compulsive, with drivers motivated by a castration complex and rebellion against their fathers."

I'm not sure I would agree with these abstract opinions, but race car drivers definitely have an unusual mental makeup. Understanding the driver's mental abilities—the positives and negatives—can help both coach and driver figure out areas that are weaknesses and work to improve their performance.

Mental Power Generation

In order to understand your capabilities, you need to maximize the return on your mental capacity. Picture your mental capacity as being like a power generator. If your generator has a capacity of 20,000 watts and during a hot and difficult race you start to need 25,000 watts, the "lights" that are plugged in and powered will start to dim, and the capacity needed to power any new requirements will not be there. The fuse will blow, and everything will be shut down. When this happens, a race car is probably flying off the road backward.

The key for any competitive race car driver is to have at least enough capacity in your personal generator to be competitive. The champions usually have excess capacity that allows them to be able to process more inputs when necessary without going into overload.

You can change your mental capacity, and you can work to extract maximum performance from it. Everyone is different in this area, but the key here is to pay attention to what works for you. Think about your best races, the ones where your focus and ability were at the top of your game. What did you do to prepare for that race? What was your mental state before the race? What can you do to reach that state again?

One way you can maximize return on mental capacity is with physical conditioning. If you are not physically strong enough to compete at the most difficult time of a race, you will begin to become distracted and draw upon the mental capacity power generator for support. If there is no spare capacity, and your physical exhaustion begins to manifest itself through slower reflexes and/or even mistakes, the car starts to get ahead of the driver as opposed to the other way around. When the race car is ahead of the driver, the driver no longer controls his environment. His environment is being controlled by his circumstances (too tired, too hot, mentally drained), and that is the danger zone for a driver.

If you are a superb, physically prepared athlete and not particularly physically challenged in the race car during a hot and difficult event, you will have that spare mental capacity available to be used for other challenges. You might use that power to focus on race strategy and how to position yourself for the best possible chance to win, or to log critical setup/performance information that you can then pass on to your race engineers.

Champions often display great mental capacity and the ability to stay ahead of the race car. Champions that have exhibited great mental capacity during races are Fernando Alonso, Mario Andretti, Sébastian Bourdais, Gil de Ferran, Jeff Gordon, Michael Schumacher, and Indy 500 winners Rick Mears and Dan Wheldon.

Human Performance International

For more than 20 years in America, Human Performance International (HPI) has measured the physical and mental attributes of world-class race car drivers. HPI was founded 20 years ago by the late Dr. Dan Marisi and his colleague Dr. Jacques Dallaire, two professors with doctorates in sports psychology and sports physiology from McGill University in Montreal. I was one of the first Formula One drivers to be tested by them. I remain connected to their ways and beliefs to this day.

Working from their tests on many of the top drivers and from the credible literature on the subject, HPI assembled the Psychological Profile of Racers.

Formula One drivers are stimulus addicts, or sensation seekers, and they are certainly not men hell-bent on self-destruction. They are unusually ambitious and self-confident, easily bored, relatively intolerant of routine, and tough-minded to the extent that they have unusually low needs for intimate personal relationships and conformity. Though perhaps low on sentiment, they have high needs for attention from the opposite sex—bad news for Freudians, good news for Formula One groupies.

A constant frustration for Dr. Jacques Dallaire has been the realization that most racers aren't terribly concerned with their mental condition. "Drivers spend hours and hours training themselves physically," he says, "yet the majority of their performance ability is defined by their mental strengths."

Mental Toughness

Formula One world champion Nigel Mansell is a superb example of a driver with so much belief in himself that he needed very little emotional support from a team. Throughout his racing career, no matter what happened, he was able to brush it off and move on to the next level. Mansell was my teammate in the European Formula Two Championship in Donington

Park, England, in 1978. He failed to even qualify for the race because his car was sub-par. He simply absorbed this blow to his ego and moved on.

Few people believed that Mansell would ever make it to the big time. He proved over and over again, however, that he just might be mentally the toughest driver I have ever known.

When he drove for my old team, Williams Grand Prix, he blossomed and didn't care what they thought of his quirky behavior. All he wanted from them was the best car on the grid, which they gave him, and he went on to become world champion with a spectacular season in 1992. He did all this in a team that was emotionally cold and known for not emotionally supporting its drivers.

Emotionally Vulnerable

Other talented Formula One drivers did not flourish in the Williams team's emotionally cold atmosphere. German Formula One driver Heinz-Harald Frentzen has always needed far more emotional support than Nigel Mansell. During his time at Williams, his true talent became buried under emotional distractions and pressures and the team's doubts of his abilities, which resulted in Frentzen second-guessing himself. It got so bad that Frentzen could not perform at peak performance, and although he was a winner at Williams, he eventually got fired. When he moved to Jordan Grand Prix, a team that nurtures drivers, Frentzen flourished and went on to have his finest days in Formula One, winning several Grands Prix and almost winning the world championship in 1999.

Consider the fact that Heinz-Harald Frentzen and Michael Schumacher are both Germans who developed their racing skills in karts and Formula Three. Both were signed into the Mercedes-Benz young-driver development program, and both drove the Mercedes Group C car in the World Sport car championship.

There was a time when some people believed Frentzen was actually faster than Schumacher. When both drivers made it to Formula One, Schumacher's superior mental skills left Frentzen in the dust. Schumacher had no interest in other drivers, in their speed or in their overall performance. He had total confidence in his own abilities and focused every moment on working to improve himself and his car. The intense pressure of Formula One was easy to absorb for Schumacher.

Frentzen on the other hand enjoyed himself driving for the Sauber Formula One team and developed well. Sauber is well-known for its friendly and supportive atmosphere. The pressure increased immensely when Frentzen went to drive for Williams Formula One. The pressure proved to be too much, and his progress stopped. In fact, his career almost ended until he was rescued by Jordan Grand Prix.

Do you know what type of emotional support you like? In what type of emotional environment did you thrive as a child?

What are your emotional and mental hot buttons? Are you a family-supported type of individual? Do you perform well when your family is there to support you? Do you perform better when you were away from your immediate family? These types of questions will lead you to discover the type of mental environment in which you will thrive in.

Do you think that race teams know and understand what type of emotional support a driver needs? Frankly, it has been my experience that most teams have no idea about mental and emotional environments.

Do you know how to get yourself into the environment you need in order to flourish? How strong mentally do you think you are? Can you withstand the distractions of life and always perform at peak performance?

Never forget that you are what you believe. Your behavior is a byproduct of your belief system. When distracted or emotionally disturbed, you can be transferred from that state by the renewing of your mind. In other words, you need to think differently. You need to think good, positive things about yourself. Lasting change occurs in the mind first. Great drivers can always renew their minds and become the drivers they believe they are.

Circumstances dictate the mental state of many drivers, but unfortunately circumstances are always subject to change. Circumstances dictate your emotions and are always in a state of flux. Never allow circumstances to dictate your behavior.

Your belief system needs to be based on truth and not on circumstances. However, if you do not act on what you believe, which is hopefully the truth, you flounder and continue to be dictated by your circumstances and therefore by your emotional state.

Heinz-Harald Frentzen is a reactive driver who is guided by his mental state. Exterior circumstances have a profound effect on his emotional state, and he is always in a state of change. Overly reactive people are constantly being driven by their insecurities and fears.

Schumacher on the other hand was not controlled by his circumstances; he had a strong belief system that drove him and kept him level. You are what you think; Michael Schumacher is what he thinks, and Heinz-Harald Frentzen is what he thinks.

Respected journalist Mark Hughes had an interesting take on mental strength. Hughes believed that although all competitive sports require mental strength, motorsports is at the extreme end of the scale. It's more complex than most sports and more dangerous. As well as the concern about achieving your own maximum competitive performance, there's the complex matrix of the car to consider, all against a subconscious backdrop of self-preservation.

"Uncertainty is the enemy of getting in the zone. That and emotion, but emotion's a strange one, a dangerous force in that it can be used to tease out depths of performance, but can just as easily turn on you," Hughes explains. "I've always felt that the way for someone to beat Michael would be to create doubt in his mind.

"Michael's incredibly mentally strong, and that was shown clearly in 1996 when he had a dog of a car but still won races. It's so easy in that situation to get yourself into a spiral of negativity that affects your performance.

"Jacques Villeneuve plays mind games with weaker teammates. Heinz-Harald Frentzen and Ricardo Zonta came away bruised. There are stories that during Zonta's time at BAR, Jacques would throw the rookie's dinner in the bin if he was late arriving."

Villeneuve's friend Olivier Panis wasn't impressed with the dinner-tossing stunt. "If he did that to me," Panis said, "I'd smash his face in!"

Nigel Mansell was one of Formula One's most exciting and aggressive drivers, yet he did not need big doses of emotional support from the team. For him, it was almost as if the performances were rooted in proving everyone wrong. Unusually, Mansell seemed to use his paranoia in a positive way.

Senna had the persona of a warrior. He seemed to thrive in a war zone. Senna, in fact, was one of the very few who took that dangerous partner, emotion, and danced with it. Tragically, it probably killed him, just as it did Gilles Villeneuve.

Jackie Stewart used to describe how he would try to "deflate like a balloon" before he got in the car, to drain himself of all emotion so he could operate with cold, clinical precision. Finns Mika Hakkinen and Kimi Raikkonen seem to be utterly devoid of emotion anywhere near a car.

It's clear when looking at this subject that there are as many different types of mental strength as there are drivers. It's also apparent that traits that are strengths in certain situations are flaws in others. Where there's no room for doubt, how do you rationalize defeat? How do you find room to improve? But when you acknowledge the scope to get better, how do you prevent awkward questions creeping in about the strengths of others? How do you prevent yourself conspiring to let them defeat you? Questions, always questions. The really tough guys answer them, then forget them. The others hold them at bay.

Mario Andretti—the 1978 Formula One world champion—is a man who has seen it all. His words are well respected. He was once quoted as saying he believed that, "Not too many people know how to win. A lot of people know how to go fast, and they'll be a factor, but knowing how to win is knowing how to control your emotions. I see drivers who are quick, they'll be up front for a while, but you know they'll never win. They'll make a mistake, they'll do something that will cause them not to be there in the end. They just don't have the capacity, the capability, to have that mental strength."

Indy car champion and Indy 500 winner Dan Wheldon has proven many times that he has the mental capacity to win consistently. He understands what it takes to win. He is very good at knowing how and where to position himself for the best opportunity to win. He has the skills to go fast, but he also has the mental capacity to know how to win.

THE YOUNG AND THE RESTLESS

In 1996 and 1997, during our Team Green Academy driver-development program at Derek Daly Performance Driving Academy, we had a fascinating insight into the physical, and more importantly, the mental makeup of 46 fine young American drivers. The two drivers who were chosen for support, Jeff Shafer and Matt Sielsky, could do about the same lap time, but they differed dramatically in strengths and weaknesses, particularly when it came to mental strength. Although they were not the most complete drivers during our evaluations, their potential for the future was the reason they were targeted for coaching and development.

When we looked back over the years of notes on each driver, it also became very apparent that the drivers' traits, both strong and weak, became visible almost immediately. The ones with strong mental skills always had an air of confidence and a sense of security and presence about them. The drivers who did not possess strong mental skills were consistently making excuses at every opportunity and did not have that air of confidence. Remember, drivers with both weak and strong mental skills can do about the same lap times in certain conditions, but only strong mental skills will consistently withstand the distractions and pressures of professional racing at the Formula One and Indy car levels.

For the 1997 season, our two drivers set off on their development program. Jeff Shafer had superb mental skills and therefore his personal performance was never dictated by his circumstances. He had an unshakable belief in his own abilities. His weakness was his understanding of the technical side of a racing car.

Matt Sielsky did not have the same unshakable belief in his own abilities, and his personal performance was constantly dictated by his circumstances. We all agreed that Sielsky was very gifted and had superb natural talent, in addition to a good basic understanding of the technical side of a racing car. His weakness, however, was that he was emotionally fragile.

As we coached and developed their skills during the following two seasons, and because we concentrated on developing their individual weaknesses, we took a vastly different approach to each individual driver.

Most of the focus for Shafer was to develop his technical skills because his mental skills were already strong. He was placed with a team that ran a unique Nemesis F2000 chassis that no one else in the field had. This decision alone would be enough to sidetrack many drivers, however, our reasoning was that it would force Shafer to think and learn how to make his individual car fast, and he would not be tempted to become an eyeball engineer. Eyeball engineers tend to try to take the easy way out when it comes to setup decisions. They want what they see on other cars rather than working through the setup process as it is meant to be. It was important for Shafer's development that this option was not available to him, as it would speed up his learning process.

During the season, he displayed his superior mental strength many times because he had virtually no interest in other drivers, their lap times, or their cars. The only thing that interested him was the performance of his car, and that was what he focused on constantly. The circumstances created by what other drivers did were only of passive interest to him.

For Matt Sielsky, we had little interest in the technical side of his racing car because, quite frankly, it didn't matter how fast his car was; if he became mentally distracted, he would fly off the road anyway.

Sielsky's program was focused on teaching him *how* to win. He had the same Van Diemen F2000 chassis as everyone else (except Jeff Shafer) because that immediately removed any questionable variable about his equipment compared to his main competitors. Sielsky's technical skills at this stage in his career were also quite good, so we did not need him to think technically outside the box.

Sadly, after two seasons, we never could pierce his personal wall of doubt. Sielsky's superb natural talent made it easy for him to qualify on the pole, set fastest race laps, and set new lap records. When it came to winning, he always seemed to fall short. All through the seasons, he was constantly worried about the speed of other drivers. He was consumed by how he looked and what people thought of him. And in the presence of his father, his whole countenance would change. It became a real struggle to get him to believe in himself and to concentrate and focus on winning. His circumstances dictated his behavior and his performance.

At the end of the second season, Sielsky had made no progress in developing his mental skills and continued to have a very shaky foundation. Consequently, the next higher step up the ladder of his career, Toyota Atlantic, proved too much for him to handle.

Shafer, meanwhile, with our lone ranger approach to teaching him the technical side of racing, went on to become a winner in that first season, and the following season he moved up to Toyota Atlantic and again performed like a star. We put him into one of the most difficult environments for an inexperienced driver—a street circuit in Vancouver, Canada. Against the established stars, Shafer qualified on the pole and led the race like a seasoned champion. He had such faith in his own abilities that faster race cars never fazed him; it was easy for him to move up.

Many times throughout his career, CART Champ Car champion Jimmy Vasser displayed great mental strength. When Vasser drove for Chip Ganassi Racing, his teammates were two highly touted drivers, Alex Zanardi and Juan Montoya. A mentally fragile driver would have been completely overwhelmed by being paired with stars like those two, but Vasser was able to ignore the distraction and focus on being the best he could be.

Vasser won the CART Champ Car championship in 1996 with a disciplined display of consistent driving powered by his mental strength. He believed in himself and performed the same way consistently no matter who his teammates were. If he wasn't able to control his emotions over the course of an entire season, he might never have become a champion.

Like him or not, a driver who has consistently displayed great mental strength is Ireland's Eddie Irvine. Throughout his early career, Irvine's belief in himself was somewhat arrogant. When he prepared to enter Formula One in 1992, he treated the event almost with disdain. He was part of a famous incident at the Japanese Grand Prix when Ayrton Senna was trying to lap him. Irvine had no interest in showing any level of respect, and the resulting on-track action by Irvine caused Senna to seek him out after the race to scold him. Irvine's arrogant attitude toward the world champion resulted in a fistfight.

For the next 10 years of his Formula One career, while Irvine drove for teams like Jordan, Jaguar, and Ferrari, he continued to show the same level of arrogance. This didn't always earn him friends, but he did display an amazing ability to avoid becoming mentally distracted by other drivers or his circumstances. Irvine provoked people by his comments and actions, but he never allowed himself to be provoked. He used his words to distract his opposition, but their response, no matter how acrid, was not allowed to penetrate his mental moat. People loved or hated Irvine, but he never cared one way or the other.

Former British karting star Jenson Button is a great example of a driver who appears to have strong mental skills. After just one season in the British Formula Three championship he was thrown straight into F1 with the Williams F1 team. The car suited his style, and he had a superb rookie season. Because Williams already had Juan Montoya under contract, the team had to loan out Button to the Renault team for his second season.

The Renault was nowhere near as good a car, and Button struggled all season long. The team manager for Renault, the flamboyant Italian Flavio Briatore, began to publicly criticize Button and actually said that if he did not improve during the 2002 season, he would be out of F1. Button had also drawn public criticism from many sides about his lavish spending and his playboy lifestyle.

With this type of scrutiny and public criticism, in addition to the intense pressure of Formula One, Button could have easily buckled under the pressure. However, as all great drivers do, his personal belief system allowed him to block out all the distractions, and he had a great 2002 season. His most important test was not whether he could sort out a race car or whether he could drive it fast, it was whether he could mentally succeed while being fed on by the piranhas of Formula One.

Button used his 2002 season to display all his talents and skills in front of a critical media and interested team owners. After surviving the test and proving his strong mental skills by withstanding that type of pressure, Button had assured himself of his place in Formula One.

In the 2003 season, Button was paired with French Canadian Jacques Villeneuve. Villeneuve was always regarded as one of the toughest of drivers mentally. Villeneuve was a master at destabilizing his teammates. He would use subtle personal attacks to try to get the upper hand off the track, which in turn could be to his advantage on the track.

When Button was announced as Villeneuve's teammate at the start of the 2002 season, Villeneuve immediately said he did not respect Button and would not respect him until he did some good things on the track. His mental pressure was relentless and designed to destabilize Button. Button withstood the pressure and spotlight and went on to outshine the 1997 world champion, Villeneuve

One of the relative newcomers against Button during the 2003 season was Finland's Kimi Raikkonen. Raikkonen is one of the most unusual drivers to appear on the scene for many years. He appears to be emotionally cold and unaffected by his surroundings. He is affectionately called the "Ice Man." Amazingly, when he reached the top by winning a

Grand Prix, he stunned many by considering the win to be no big deal.

A story in *Formula 1 Racing* magazine at the end of 2003 again highlighted the Ice Man when he was asked what winning that first Grand Prix really meant. "Nothing, really," was his flippant response. "I guess it makes you know you can win, that's the only thing. . . . It doesn't make you half a second quicker, just a bit more confident. Maybe you know you can win races when you have a good package and a good day, but that's about it."

This response shocked most people who have blood running through their veins. His reaction was a stark contrast to Rubens Barrichello, who was in tears on the podium when he won his first Grand Prix in Germany. Raikkonen's emotional coldness has shown itself to be an advantage when under severe pressure.

Whatever driver one might profile as an example of what to do or not to do, there is always one standout in the admiration column, and that is again Michael Schumacher, who never allowed himself to become visibly discouraged or depressed. Whenever Schumacher (who exhibited great mental strength) was compared to the great Ayrton Senna by Senna's team owner Frank Williams, especially in the area of mental strength, Frank always voiced that Senna "had astonishing mental preparation." When you get comments like this from team owners who have actually employed these drivers, it further emphasizes that the great champions have great mental capacity. They are all a little different, but they all possess a strong mental quality.

American sensation Danica Patrick also possesses considerable inner belief and mental strength. She needs it, as she is partly judged by the results on the track but also on how she lives her life and behaves in general. The media wants to judge her and hopes to find her guilty of something that will sell a story line. Absorbing this type of scrutiny and dealing with it without letting it become a performance-robbing distraction can create an intrigue around a personality.

All these real-life stories simply prove that some drivers can and some drivers can't overcome the mental distractions of motorsports at the top level.

If that skill is not already part of your mental makeup, you can learn it by first recognizing what it is and then starting to renew your mind. My wife Rhonda's favorite saying is "renewing of the mind," and it is a powerful step forward for everybody no matter what they do in life.

You can do the very same by believing in yourself. Move away from distractions that affect your performance. Surround yourself with positive and supportive people. Because life in general has many distractions, develop the habit and skill of renewing your mind. It will clear the road for you to display all of your natural talents every time you step into competition. Just look around you, and you can tell who makes the mistakes and who does not. Make sure you are the one who is considered solid. You are what you believe about yourself.

HOW TO DEVELOP THE MENTAL STRENGTH OF A CHAMPION

Before we get into this subject, please don't fear the admission that you might need help in this area. If you do, believe me, the quicker you admit that you could benefit from strengthening your mental muscle, the quicker you will become more effective in a race car.

What if mental strength is a weakness that needs to be boosted in a driver, just like it was with me? Where would you go; what might you do? The first thing to do is to be quietly honest with yourself and admit that it is an area that you would like to strengthen. Then seek help from a professional.

Virtually all high-performance people acknowledge that 80 percent of the game is mental, whether we are talking about a professional golfer, an Olympic athlete, a SWAT team specialist, a company CEO, or a top salesman. They recognize that it is not their physical prowess or their knowledge that ensures success in the competitive world in which they live and work, but rather that their personal success is most influenced by the mental skills they are able to bring to bear on the tasks they undertake on a day-to-day basis and during major events in their lives (the big tournament, competition, meeting, deal, etc.).

They have come to recognize that the brain is a muscle. It is the most powerful weapon in your arsenal, and you need to exercise it and train it in order to achieve and maintain peak performance.

In the past, the majority of athletes have focused time and energy only on the development or training of the physical self, with little attention paid to the development of basic mental skills. That's because tools have not been available that could effectively teach you how to focus and concentrate. Sports psychologists and coaches can provide you with tools that can help on this front (see the appendix for a listing of these resources).

COACHING PATTERNS

When you are at the top of your game, you are performing "in the zone," as they say in the sporting world. The top sporting professionals can perform consistently at that level. Superior mental focus enables them to raise their game even higher when they need to.

In order to get to the top, more and more athletes are recognizing the importance of mental as well as physical coaching. They are using the most advanced coaching technologies available today, such as neuro-linguistic programming (NLP), to achieve positive mental attitude and focus. In a nutshell, NLP is the science and art of modeling and replicating behaviors of excellence. The same coaching techniques are being applied even more powerfully within the business arena. You can enjoy the benefits of changing your own limiting behavior patterns and developing new strategies that will consistently achieve successful results for you and your business.

The role of the coach is to facilitate the changes that you want to make in yourself by supporting you with the most advanced techniques and processes that will be most effective in generating the results you want.

If you want to get to the top, stay at the top, or just enjoy being at the top of your game, then can you afford not to stack the odds in your favor?

HABITUAL BEHAVIOR PATTERNS

We behave in fairly predictable, repeatable ways. The ways we communicate, organize, delegate, and make decisions are based on patterns of behavior. For example, the complex skill of driving a race car is made up of observation, planning, decision-making, and physical-control skills, which when assembled together, enable you to drive at high speed safely while thinking about many other things at the same time—it is a learned pattern of automatic or unconscious behavior.

Bear in mind that you learned these behavior patterns when you were quite young. Strategies that were effective during your education and early working life are what you are using in your career and business today. Even if your situation has changed radically, you are most likely still using techniques that worked when you were young. Are these the most effective for you today in the competitive environment where you now reside? Probably not. And if you ask yourself, "How do I do these tasks?" you probably don't even know. Coaching works because it enables you to discover where your skills are optimal and where there are behavior patterns that are limiting your performance at the moment.

If you decide that a personal coach is for you, there are some basic steps you will have to take. The first step of the process is to establish a goal for yourself as the outcome of the coaching. This goal will enable you to measure your own performance and that of your coach against a specific, achievable objective. As long as you are positively and congruently motivated toward that goal, you will be guaranteed to achieve an excellent result. By clearly specifying your outcome, you will discover the key resources or behavior patterns that you need to improve.

The second step is to discover how well your existing strategies work, where they are successful, and most importantly, where they fail to deliver the results you want. Within the NLP framework, there are simple ways to discover what these limiting behavior patterns are and where they emanate from.

The final step is to develop new strategies that will enable you to achieve a level of performance to consistently deliver the results you want. Your coach will work with you as you implement the new behavior patterns that may help you explore some exciting new opportunities.

HOW COACHING WORKS

Anyone who is trying to develop a set of skills or a machine to perform at the highest level uses the same basic concepts. This process applies to developing a championship-winning Formula One racing car driver, perfecting a pro's golf swing, or improving a pro tennis player's serve.

Whatever the process or skill, improvement is a result of breaking down that process into its component parts. Each part is then carefully evaluated in order to discover what is working really well and which individual elements are problematic. Once you identify problem areas, you can begin to change the way the complex skills are assembled and delivered.

In the case of your own behavior patterns, the components might be your beliefs, the decisions you have made during your lifetime, your values, your motivating factors, your fears, and your learned habits. Once you have discovered how the picture fits together, change is possible. The role of the coach is to show you how to incorporate those changes in simple stages. When done well, this can be an enlightening experience.

You will be able to put your new skills into practice between coaching sessions. Each time you see your coach, you can evaluate the results and get feedback that will enable you to maintain focus and achieve your goal. The coach will also provide you with some techniques to take away and use yourself so that you will continue your own development at your own pace and enjoy the benefits of a sound investment in yourself for many years to come.

Unlike developing physical skill, mental skill development is a more difficult task because it is somewhat intangible. You can't really touch it or feel it, but you certainly can see it when it's present. Strong mental skills are essential to building the Champion's Pyramid, and strong mental skills can be a learned trait.

CHAPTER 6

PHYSICAL FITNESS

When the doctors viewed the results, they were shocked. I had the highest sustained heartbeat of any athlete they had ever measured during competition.

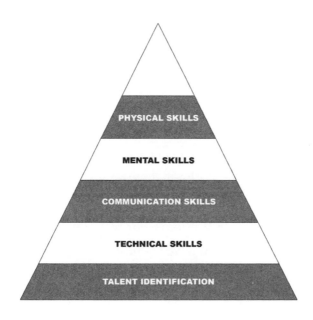

Although races early in a career are relatively short events, they still require a certain level of physical fitness, which provides a foundation for the future. Someday, you might be driving heavy cars for two or three hours, or you may compete in an endurance race like the Le Mans 24 hours.

Many people see a driver behind the wheel and have no idea that considerable physical effort must be put forth to achieve optimum performance from the vehicle. I have experienced everything physically in a race car. I have finished Grand Prix races fresh and alert, and I have also collapsed from exhaustion. I have dealt with all sorts of pain, particularly cramps, and during a grueling time in my career when I suffered physical difficulties on a regular basis, I had reason to question my own training routine. Through it all, I learned the basics about physical readiness to drive race cars.

Achieving physical fitness is very unique to each individual. Each body's metabolism works in a unique way, and it is very important to be aware of your metabolism. For example, I would perspire a lot when in a race car; therefore, I needed a lot of liquid replenishment loaded with minerals. Other drivers, such as Michael Schumacher, never look sweaty or exhausted after a race. Former Williams Formula One driver Thierry Boutsen would not even have his hair out of place after a race, whereas I regularly looked pale-faced and sometimes physically wrecked.

I clearly remember during the closing stages of the 1982 U.S. Grand Prix at Caesar's Palace in Las Vegas, I was so physically drained with five laps to go that I began to experience dizzy spells under braking. If the race had gone on much longer, I could well have gone off the road because I was so exhausted.

My metabolism could easily become mineral deficient. At the end of long hard races, I would be ashen-faced, with my eyes sunken, and just about everything would cramp easily. I would even have difficulty talking properly because my ear drums felt like they were closed off.

Immediately after the Spanish Grand Prix in 1980, I was so dehydrated that as soon as I got out of the car, I began to gulp down a large bottle of iced water. The shock of the cold water to my dehydrated body caused me to go dizzy and collapse. As I began to fall, I called out to fellow driver and future teammate, Keke Rosberg. I woke up with Rosberg pounding on my chest in a state of panic because he thought my heart had stopped. I was taken to the medical center where an IV replenished the fluids, and I quickly recovered.

In 1984, the Hovik Medical Group from San Diego monitored my heartbeat during the Long Beach Grand Prix. Over the course of the two hours, I averaged 178 beats per minute with a high of 199 beats per minute. When the doctors viewed the results, they were shocked. I had the highest sustained heartbeat of any athlete they had ever measured during competition. This was during a time when race car drivers were not really regarded as true athletes because driving cars (particularly on television) looks somewhat easy.

The doctors realized that a race car cockpit is a hostile environment that taxes the human body more than most athletic endeavors in the world. Professional race car drivers wear two layers of fireproof underwear and three layers of a fireproof driving suit. They then put on a balaclava, a helmet, and gloves and close the helmet visor, which restricts the flow of cool fresh oxygen needed to cool an athlete's body. It is one of the most restrictive environments an athlete can be subjected to while being expected to perform at a world-class level. World-class cyclists are the only other athletes in the world with similar sustained high heartbeats.

PHYSICAL CONTROL THROUGH THE MIND

During the 1988 Le Mans 24-hour race, I was driving for the biggest team there: Jaguar. I was part of a five-car assault and a multi million–dollar attack to try to win the most prestigious endurance race in the world. Our car finished fourth, with our sister car winning. During the race, I have vivid memories of severe cramps in my legs and feet at 3 a.m. as I stood in the pit lane with my seat back in hand, ready to get in to do a two-hour double stint. That was when I learned that my state of mind could affect me physically.

REALITY OF THE GYM

Let me tell you the truth about working out to get ready to drive a race car. I don't care how much training you do in the gym or what level of personal trainer you have; you will not become totally race fit without being in the race car, actually experiencing the activity. You simply cannot replicate the g forces exerted on the body while at speed no matter what type of exercise you do. After a long layoff, or when driving a bigger car for the first time, your forearms, wrists, and neck will ache until those body parts raise their tolerance as you get more mileage in that type of car. You can, however, use the gym to make your body strong enough to adapt more quickly to the rigors of driving a race car.

Why should peak physical conditioning be a requirement? Well, it wasn't as necessary in my days in Formula One (1978–1982). Mario Andretti and Niki Lauda never bothered with workouts. Andretti would never spend his youth in a gym, and Niki Lauda never looked anything more than an average physical specimen, yet they both won world championships.

Today, the bar has been raised, particularly by Michael Schumacher. Did you ever see Michael Schumacher look physically drained after a race? It was not too long ago that Ayrton Senna had to be lifted from his car at the end of a Grand Prix. Another three-time Formula One world champion, Nelson Piquet, collapsed on the podium after winning his home Grand Prix in Brazil. Their physical fitness at that time was just about enough to get the job done, but today it is all very different. Today, every discipline from karts to Formula One is more competitive. If you have an equal kart with the rest of the field, your physical conditioning can make the difference between winning and being part of the rest of the field.

Remember that as your physical strength decreases during a race, your mental capacity begins to diminish, and your opportunity to make mistakes increases. Being in peak physical shape will help you stay mentally sharp during the race.

During the Le Mans 24-hour race with Jaguar in 1988, I discussed my cramping dilemma with the team trainer, Tom Ryan. At that time in my career, muscle cramping had become more of an issue. I began to increase my workouts to raise my tolerance level. Ryan asked to see my workout routine and, after studying it carefully, he simply said that I needed to cut my workouts at least by half. He said that I was too tired to drive effectively and that my extensive workout routine was not giving my body enough time to rest and rejuvenate. That was a very interesting lesson. I stopped working out for the rest of the season, got stronger, and my mid-race cramping was gone.

Another reason for physical fatigue in a race car is not being relaxed. Instead of treating the steering with a delicate touch, some drivers hang on with a white-knuckle grip that taxes their bodies much more. World champion Nigel Mansell would grip the steering wheel of the Williams F1 car tightly and manhandle the car to the point that he would be physically and mentally exhausted after a race.

When I drove for the Jaguar team at Le Mans, we had a steering sensor that would document which drivers used more physical input through the steering to do the same lap time. The high-physical-input drivers would also wear out the steering joints faster than a driver with a delicate touch. Coincidently, the drivers with high physical input through the steering column would be harder on the brakes and would use more tires and fuel to do the same lap time.

RELAX AND ENJOY

A relaxed driving position with deep breathing and a delicate touch on the steering wheel is much more efficient. Not every driver is naturally inclined to drive this way. However, the more aware you are of this style, the more likely you will be to use it to your advantage. I know this works, because I forced myself to drive the Jaguar like this in Le Mans, and I could do a two-hour stint, at speeds up to 250 miles per hour, on the verge of cramping but without losing time or position on the track.

READING YOUR BODY

Tuning for optimum physical fitness is very much like tuning the kart or race car for optimum performance. Just as the car will tell you what it wants or needs, your body will do exactly the same. It is your job (with the help of a personal trainer) to read all the messages accurately and act upon the needs as required. If you make mistakes with the setup of the car, you will pay the price. If you make mistakes with your physical conditioning, you will also pay the price.

If you perspire a lot like I did, carefully read the situation and make sure you pre-hydrate and replenish as often as possible with mineral-loaded drinks. Turn your food into useful strength and energy by giving your body good nourishment. Alcohol stays in your bloodstream for up to 48 hours, so think about whether you want to compromise your abilities in any way by drinking too much alcohol the night before a race.

Whatever muscle group gets sore while driving, work on those muscles specifically. In 1982, my Formula One teammate, Keke Rosberg, elected not to work out his neck muscles; instead, he tied his helmet to both sides of the cockpit, which allowed him to withstand the g forces of the Williams FW08 and keep his head upright. Rosberg won the world championship that year, but that type of casual physical preparation would not suffice today (Rosberg was also a smoker, drinker, and womanizer).

Whenever you can make the driving position more comfortable or cooler, do it. Most of all, the biggest way to save physical strength is to drive in a relaxed and efficient mode.

Examples of drivers who were cool, calm, and relaxed in the race car are Niki Lauda (a three-time world champion), Katherine Legge, and John Watson (a five-time Grand Prix winner). Sometimes, you may have to coax yourself into this mode while driving and find the rhythm that you need to be energy efficient *and* fast.

If you want to be a champion in the mold of a Michael Schumacher, he has already set the bar. In order to reach that height, you need to have first-class physical conditioning.

SPECIALIZED TRAINING

You can go to any reputable gym in any country and find a very good trainer who will put you in the best physical shape of your life. However, because motorsports makes unusual physical demands on the body, if you are aiming for the top, you will be better off choosing a trainer who specializes in training a race car driver.

One such person is Jim Leo, owner of PitFit Training in Indianapolis. Leo has a wealth of knowledge and experience with race car drivers, and if I were to set myself a specific target, I would like to have someone beside me who could "aim" me in the right direction.

I have included a section penned by Leo himself that accurately sets a driver on the right path in preparing to endure the physical rigors of racing at high speed.

A FITNESS PROGRAM FOR RACERS
BY JIM LEO

Preseason Fitness Preparation

For many drivers, off-season fitness consists of tearing down an engine or watching *American Idol* on television. The question you must ask yourself is whether or not you want to make an impact on your racing season before it even begins.

Gaining an edge on the competition by improving fitness is an aspect of racing in which every driver should take interest. Drivers from all levels of racing have discovered greater success in racing performance by following a structured fitness program. Before you get started, you need to understand the basic fitness components and why improving them will improve your driving skill.

Endurance

Research has shown that driver heart rates average 152 beats per minute in an Indy-style race car on a road course. At PitFit Training, we have measured heart rates as high as 196 beats per minute with a 29-year-old driver in a 125-cc shifter kart. In similar research, we have found an average of 170 beats per minute for a full 10-minute stint in the same type of kart. These were not overweight, out-of-shape drivers but six healthy drivers in their 20s and 30s. These heart rates compare to those of competitive endurance athletes, such as cyclists and runners. If you think racing karts does not heavily tax the cardiovascular system, think again. Then think of what it might be like if you progress to racing big, heavy cars like Formula One, Champ Cars, stock cars, or Indy cars.

Strength

The idea of lifting weights to improve on-track performance may surprise some drivers. Strength training, especially in the shoulder and torso region, will reduce the amount of fatigue felt as the race progresses and will allow the driver to maintain better control of the race car. It is apparent that a driver lacks the strength to race at peak levels when he can't consistently stay in the proper groove in corners and begins missing apexes he was successfully driving through earlier in the race. These mistakes often cause a driver to lose positions in the closing laps.

Reaction Times

Many year's ago, the U.S. military discovered that soldiers who played reaction-based video games performed better on combat drills requiring fast reflexes. Video games that require instant processing of thoughts train the brain in a similar fashion to what a driver experiences in a kart. Should you quit your job and saddle up next to the geek at the local game shop playing the latest edition of Forza? No, but playing games that stimulate the mind to process information and immediately react to this information might improve how well you react on track.

Flexibility

One of the most controversial topics in modern sports conditioning is whether or not stretching positively affects athletic performance. Except in certain cases, professionals now believe that stretching doesn't help most athletes. Research has shown that an athlete should focus on warm-up motions similar to the sport in which they participate. Properly warming up a particular part of the body increases heat production, thus increasing the range of motion. One would be hard pressed to find many sports asking an athlete to hold a position for 20–30 seconds followed by a rest period. Taking the body through a series of warm-up movements not only warms up the body but also slowly raises the heart rate. This gradual progression better prepares the athlete for the demands of competition. Without a warm-up, some blood that should be assisting to transport much-needed oxygen to the lungs may instead be redirected to warm up cold muscles.

Testing

What is testing? The repetitive analysis of performance in a controlled environment. In race car or kart testing, this data can be used to determine progress and to make adjustments. If you would take the money and time to spend a day testing your race car or kart, why would you not use the same scientific approach with your body?

Developing a simple fitness testing protocol will provide the driver a baseline of information on current fitness levels as well as provide goals to work toward. Choose one or two basic tests from each category in the following list and retest yourself monthly to evaluate progress. It is important to precisely follow the exact protocol at each test.

Cardiovascular Measures

1- or 3-mile run time
- Use either indoor or outdoor track; run distance as fast as possible.

2,000 meters on rowing ergometer time
- Use Concept II Ergometer to row 2,000 meters as fast as possible.

500-yard swim time
- Using 25-yard pool, swim 500 yards as fast as possible (in a 25-yard pool, swim 20 lengths).

10–minute exercise bike time trial distance
- Find a comfortable exercise bike, and choose a program that measures distance. Choose a distance goal, and ride as hard as you can.

Strength Measures

1-minute pushup reps
- This can be done on toes or knees. Start in pushup position, and with a rigid torso, drop down and touch ground with

your chin. Push back up until full elbow extension. The movement must be continuous with no pausing. Do as many as you can in one minute.

Maximum pull-up reps

- Hanging from pull-up bar with palms-forward grip, lift body until chin is even with hands. Release and continue.

Knees at 90-degree wall-sit time

- Lean back against a wall with knees bent at a 90-degree angle. Hold for as long as possible without breaking form.

Lateral core endurance time

- Lie in a side-bridge position, with legs extended and top foot placed on lower foot for support. Support yourself on one elbow and on feet while lifting hips off the floor to create a straight line over the length of the body. The uninvolved arm is held across the chest with the hand placed on the opposite shoulder. Failure occurs when you lose the straight-back posture and the hip returns to the ground.

Flexibility Measures

Seated toe-touch distance to or past toes

- In seated position on floor with legs fully extended, point fingers forward together and measure the distance from your toes, or how far past your toes your fingers extend. Score is measured as a minus if toes can't be reached and positive if they can.
- Reach-over-shoulder distance from base of neck (both arms)

- You will need assistance. Reach right arm up and back so your hand is behind your neck/back. The left arm is brought around the side and up the back. Attempt to make the hands meet behind the back and, if possible, overlap. Measure the distance between the thumbs. If there is an overlap, measure as a negative. If no overlap, measure as a positive.

Reaction Measures

"I'm a driver drill"
- How quickly you can blame your engine when you stall at the start? (Just kidding.)

Card-grab catches
- You will need assistance. Have partner stand in front of you, arm's length away. Place your own hands by your side. Holding a playing card at eye level, the partner drops the card and you attempt to catch the card. Alternate hands.

Getting Started with Your Program

In the initial installment of this progressive training program, we covered why it is important to train your body to improve performance in a race car or kart. We will now learn a fundamentally basic fitness and reaction program that will become the foundation for more advanced training programs. Though you may be shown more advanced methods of training, it's very important you follow the progression we set up. Otherwise, you will not develop the proper strength for more advanced training.

There are three areas we will cover:

1. Strength
2. Stamina (endurance)
3. Reaction

Strength Training

Strength training in order to be fit to drive is different than training to look good on the beach. A driver who is more interested in impressing others with his body will seldom be in optimal race-specific condition when the green flag drops. Training the muscles for both muscular strength and muscular endurance will provide the greatest benefit to the driver.

The primary concepts of your strength training are as follows: Focus on using individual limbs whenever possible, and utilize dumbbells, body weight, and cable machines. Work in a brisk manner between exercises to keep the heart rate elevated and reduce your ability to lift heavier loads. Use a circuit-training format in which you perform an exercise for 20 repetitions, rest for 10 seconds, then move to the next exercise in the workout. Repeat until all exercises are completed and start over. Track progress of each weight lifted, as this will allow you to make adjustments in later workouts. On each phase of an exercise, use a steady two-count. For example, when performing a bench press, you would count to two as you push the weight upward and count to two when bringing the weight back down.

There are a few reasons why we stay away from weight machines when possible: Using dumbbells ensures that regardless of where you train, the weight lifted is the same. Weight machines tend to be varied in their weight stacks, thus making it difficult to judge progress when training anywhere but your primary gym. Body weight will only change as you gain or lose weight. Thus, knowing a wide range of body-weight exercises ensures your training equipment is always with you! For the smaller driver, some weight machines won't fit the body correctly, thus increasing the chance of improper form. Using both sides of the body simultaneously can create imbalance issues because the stronger side may compensate for the weakness in opposite limb.

Breathing: There are normally two phases to a strength-training movement. One is the exertion phase, which requires the most effort. On a bench press, this is pushing the bar upward. On a rowing exercise, this is pulling the weight toward you. The other phase is the recovery phase, when the resistance is decreased as you return to the starting position. On the exertion phase, focus on exhaling. On the recovery phase, focus on inhaling. This breathing pattern increases the efficiency of the exercise and reduces problems with lightheadedness.

Speed: On both phases of a movement, focus on a steady two-count movement. For example, on a chest press, you would perform the exertion phase for two counts and the recovery phase for two counts.

Repetitions: The goal for each exercise is to achieve 20 repetitions without stopping. If you can finish with this number of reps and you feel the effort is high, you have selected a good weight. If you can do more than 20, increase the weight on the next set. If you can't do 20, you may want to decrease the amount of resistance.

Here are a number of exercises to follow for the initial phase of your strength-training program:

Cable row: In a seated position, pull the bar to your body and return to starting position. Works upper back muscles, trapezius, and rhomboids.

Crossover cable: Stand with cables at shoulder level. Keep arms in position similar to if you were hugging a barrel, and bring cables together until hands touch. Release to starting position. Works upper chest and shoulders (pectoralis major, deltoids).

Leg press: Using a standard leg press, start with knees bent at a 90-degree angle and extend legs forward until knees are almost fully extended (don't lock knees). Return to starting position. For more advanced training, lift only one side at a time. Works front legs (quadriceps) and glutes.

Dumbbell shoulder press: Stand holding dumbbells with arms at a 90-degree angle, push weights upward until they lightly touch together; return to starting position. It is important to lower the weights only to a 90-degree angle. Works shoulders (deltoids) and triceps.

Leg curl: There are different variations of this machine; use what is available. Lying face down on the machine, raise the weight all the way so your heals touch your body. Release to starting position. For more advanced training, lift only one side at a time. Works back of legs (hamstrings).

Dumbbell lateral raise: Stand, holding dumbbells at your side with your palms facing in and elbows at a 10-degree bend. Raise the weights upward to your sides until they are ear level, then return to start. Works shoulders, primarily middle deltoid.

Front raise: In the same position as the lateral raise, raise the dumbbells upward in front of your body to eye level, then release down. Hands should remain in what is called a "hammer grip." Works front portion of the shoulder (anterior deltoid).

Hammer curl: Standing in the same position as the front raise, curl weight upward by bending elbow until the weight nearly touches the front part of your shoulder, and then return down to side. Works biceps and forearm muscles.

Triceps pressdown: Stand with hands holding triceps rope or bar, elbows positioned at sides of body. Push weight downward while keeping elbows at your sides until arms are fully extended. Return to starting position. Works triceps.

Scarecrow: Stand with weights in hand, elbows at 90-degree angle with weights directly above elbows. Lower weights forward while maintaining elbows at the same position. Once you reach full range of motion, raise weights back to starting position. Works rotator cuff.

Side plank: Lying on your side on the ground, raise your body up and balance on elbow and outside of foot. Hold position for 30 seconds.

Front plank: Lying on floor facing down, elevate and balance on both elbows and toes. Hold body rigid for 30 seconds.

Toe-touch crunch: Lie on back with legs fully extended and feet high in the air. Start with shoulders flat on floor and attempt to curl up and touch the toes. Return to start. If you have back problems or experience back pain, perform the same movement but leave your feet on the floor with knees bent at 90 degrees.

Here are some strength-training exercises for weight machines:

Seated chest press: Start with elbows at 90 degrees. Exhale and push forward until arms are almost straight. Avoid locking elbows. Return to starting position.

Seated row: Chest against pad, arms should be fully extended. Pull the bar toward you until your elbows are at 90 degrees. Bring weight back to starting position.

Leg press: Start with legs on footplate, knees at 90 degrees. Push footplate forward until legs are extended but not fully locked at knees. Return to start.

Shoulder press: Start seated with feet flat on floor. Start with elbows at 90 degrees and push weight upward until nearly fully extended. Return to start.

Leg curl: In seated position with knees at 90 degrees,

pull weight toward your body. Try to get a full range of motion on this movement. Return to starting position.

Arm curl: In seated position, curl weight up toward the shoulder. Return to starting position.

Seated dip: Sit on seat with feet flat on ground, start with just above 90 degrees. Press downward until near full extension of elbows. Return to start.

Stamina Training

To properly train your body to withstand the heart-rate stress encountered when driving, you must try to simulate these same stresses in training. Performing reaction skills while the heart rate is elevated will also be important, as this is precisely what occurs when making on-track decisions in a race.

Our research has shown a driver's heart rate while racing a 125-cc kart averages between 140 and 175 beats per minute, and Derek Daly's personal heart monitoring during the Long Beach Grand Prix Champ Car race in 1983 showed an elevated heart rate of 178 beats per minute on *average* for the two-hour duration.

There are numerous types of activities you can choose for cardiovascular training, but it's important to incorporate variety. While it's often comfortable to train in one activity, this increases the risk of overuse injury. Choose one or two activities that stress opposing muscles of the lower body, like biking and running, and one that focuses on the upper body, such as swimming or rowing.

In this phase of the training, I want you to focus on two specific training zones:

Max endurance (ME): This is the foundation of your stamina training and consists of one to two hours of low-intensity training. The pace should be high enough to raise the heart rate to the 125–150 range but not so high you can't finish the desired duration. It's best to do these with low-impact activities, such as cycling or an elliptical trainer in the gym. Perform ME workout two to three times per week.

Short intervals (SI): This is a fairly short but intense series of bursts that raises the heart rate to the highest levels. Examples would be 100-meter sprints, 25 yards in the pool, etc. I only want you to do these one or two times weekly until more of a foundation of training is developed. Never do SIs on consecutive days.

Reaction Training

Performing reaction-based drills is crucial to improving on-track performance. There are dozens of drills we do with our drivers, but the fundamental principle in these drills is they are performed while the driver is in a fatigued state. Rather than provide complicated exercises, focus on a simple activity you can combine with your ME workout.

While seated on an exercise bike, play catch with a partner using a tennis ball. Have the partner alternate on which side the ball is thrown. Have your partner throw the ball toward your chest and call out which hand to use just as the ball leaves his or her hand.

Juggling: Start with one ball and simply toss from one hand and catch with the other. Repeat for one minute. Gradually work in a second ball and, if you have the talent, a third ball. Doing this when you are fresh sounds easy. Try it after a hard workout, when it's a struggle to hold your arms in front of you!

Card catch: Have a partner drop playing cards from eye level. You must start with hands at your side and alternate hands while trying to catch the card before it gets to the ground.

For each aspect of your program, I'll start you with fundamentals. For some of you with more training experience, this approach may seem too simple. Keep in mind that everything we do at PitFit Training is based on a progression that starts with the fundamentals. Patience is advised, and you will soon discover the logic behind the program.

Endurance Training

We see it all the time. Someone decides to run their first 5K race. They start jogging three times per week at a comfortable pace. Eventually, they work up to running the race distance. On race morning, the gun goes off, and they start with their fellow competitors at a speed that is faster than that at which they trained. Suddenly, at the first mile they are exhausted, now walking until they can catch their breath. They finish the race but are stunned as to why they struggled. What happened? The runner subjected himself to a workload that was harder than the training workload, and the body fatigued in response.

During a race, your heart rate will rise well above resting levels. How much it increases depends on your current fitness, conditions, and the difficulty of the track. You will need to train at various intensities throughout the program, but before you can work at higher heart-rate levels you must train longer and at a low intensity. This max endurance training is designed to strengthen your aerobic base before you launch into a more difficult anaerobic workout. Think of ME training as the foundation of your house. You can certainly have a great looking house without a solid foundation, but over time you will have problems. Building your ME will ensure fewer injuries and more efficient training as the program progresses. Plus, it's not as hard!

When implementing the ME aspect of your endurance training program, it's important to vary your modes of exercise between multiple activities. Reliance on one form of cardiovascular training can lead to injury, boredom, and ineffectiveness. The human body is quite amazing in its ability to adapt, so remember to resist the temptation to become a creature of habit. Choose three or four different activities that complement each other. This means choosing things that utilize different muscle groups, such as biking/running/swimming or rowing/elliptical trainer/boxing.

Your intensity will be low, and your duration will be long for ME workouts. Your ME workout should be at least three times the length of your race duration if the race is one hour or less. For example, if you race for 20 minutes, the ME workout will be for one hour. Races longer than one hour require 1.5 to two times the length of the race. On a scale of one to ten, with ten being the most difficult, the intensity level on ME workouts should be a five or six. Perform these workouts no more than three times per week, with at least 48 hours between workouts.

NUTRITION

A common concern for drivers is what and when they should eat and drink during race weekend. Even the most health-conscious driver will struggle to find high-performance nutritional choices at most local racetracks around the country. Unfortunately, most racetrack food stands offer fried chicken sandwiches, French fries, and other greasy foods, while racers should be eating performance foods like fruit and yogurt. The solution is to put as much planning into your weekend nutrition as you do car setup. It's simple: fail to plan . . . plan to fail. Here are some tips to assist in making sure you don't fail.

Pack: Familiar, nonperishable food. Bottled/canned drinks and drink mixes. Food you can combine to make a meal, i.e., bagel, peanut butter, banana, and juice, or tuna, crackers, apple, cheese, beef jerky, and water.

Once you arrive at your destination, go to the local grocery store and stock up on perishable foods and drinks, such as low-fat milk and milk products (yogurt, cheese, etc.) to store in a refrigerator if one is available.

Pre-Race Meal Guidelines
- Eat one to four hours before competition.
- Meals two to four hours before should be high in carbohydrates, moderate in protein, and low in fat.
- Meals eaten within one hour of competition should be high in carbohydrates, low in fiber, and low in fat.
- Avoid sugary foods before testing, qualifying, or races.

Sample Pre-Race Diet
- Two to three hours before: Moderate-sized plate of plain pasta with tomato sauce and some meatballs for protein, bottled water.
- One hour before: Energy bar or yogurt and banana, bottled water.
- Thirty minutes before: Sports drink, possibly diluted to reduce sugar density.
- Within 30 minutes: You may sip a diluted sports drink, but it's best to avoid taking in solid foods. An energy gel can be useful but should be followed by a small amount of water.

- Within 15 minutes: Nothing. To remedy dry mouth, chew on ice. Be conscious of the cleanliness of the ice to avoid potential bacterial contamination.

Between Heats and During Race

- Drink 6–12 ounces of cool fluid every 15–20 minutes (if possible).
- Eat 30–60 grams of carbohydrates (sports drinks, fruit, pretzels, or fig cookies are great snack choices).
- Eat familiar, easy-to-pack, high-carbohydrate meals between events.

Post-Race

- Eat a high-carbohydrate snack with some low-fat protein within 30 minutes. *(Try yogurt and a granola bar or peanut butter on an English muffin.)*
- Eat a high-carbohydrate, moderate-protein meal within two hours after competition.

HYDRATION

Drivers often ask what, when, and how much fluid they should consume before a race. As with any athlete, maintaining a rigid hydration schedule on race weekend can often mean the difference between running consistently at the front and fading to the rear as the race progresses. The loss of as little as 3 percent of body weight due to dehydration can impair the performance of a driver. This equates to a loss of 4.5 pounds in a 150-pound driver.

The proper hydration program actually begins two or three days prior to the first stint in the car. The driver should begin consuming additional fluids throughout the day, finding the right amount each day that promotes clear urine output but not so much that gastrointestinal issues arise. This fluid intake must be scheduled as opposed to waiting for the thirst response to tell when it is time to drink. Because there is a delay from when the driver becomes dehydrated until he becomes thirsty, it's best to consume fluids throughout the day. Water is the best choice, and it's also wise to begin limiting caffeine consumption, as too much caffeine can cause you to lose more fluid.

On each day of driving, the driver should start with 6–10 ounces of water as soon as he wakes up. This helps replenish fluids lost the previous night due to respiration. The driver should continue to drink throughout the day and during breaks from driving. Along with urine color, a simple way to determine fluid loss and replenishment is through pre- and post-stint weigh-ins. Always weigh with as little clothing as possible. For every pound of body weight lost, drink 6–8 ounces of water or a commercial sports drink.

On race day, here are fluid guidelines:
- 6–12 ounces water when driver wakes
- 16 ounces of water/sports drink two hours before event

- 4–8 ounces of water 30 minutes before event
- Chew ice only up to 10 minutes before. Make sure the ice is clean.

CHAPTER 7

DESIRE AND COMMITMENT

A true champion needs the desire to chase the dream through the most difficult of times, the desire to win at all costs, and the desire to be the best you can be at all times.

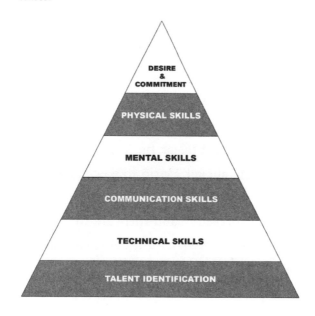

The final piece to build the Champion's Pyramid is made up of desire and commitment. Everything discussed so far is teachable, learnable, or coachable, but desire and commitment are not; they come from the heart.

Desire is a bit like a driver's blood type, except you cannot measure it with a piece of equipment. Desire is a part of the driver's heart and soul. The drive within the heart is what produces the type of desire needed to chase a motorsports dream (or any dream for that matter). A true champion needs the desire to chase the dream through the most difficult of times, the desire to win at all costs, the desire to be the best you can be at all times.

Although desire is not measurable with equipment, it is apparent in a driver's behavior. Drivers who show true desire tend to attract enthusiasts who like to support true desire. These are the types of relationships that can accelerate a career forward.

I once asked Mario Andretti what he believed was the most important thing a young driver needed when he set out to make it to the top. Was it talent, bravery, money, technical ability, or none of the above? Mario looked me in the eye and uttered just one word: desire. Because motorsports is such a hard business to succeed in and there are so many hurdles to overcome, Andretti believed that the desire to be successful was the final attribute that separated potential stars from pretenders. He said that hundreds of drivers would like to be successful, but only a small number have the desire to do whatever is necessary to chase the dream.

Strong desire to be successful often rubs people the wrong way. Strong desire needs to be surrounded by secure people who understand the actions of people with strong desire. A so-called "killer instinct" is present in most champions with a strong desire to win.

EUROPEAN MENTALITY

I grew up with the European road racing mentality and lived through many struggles before finally making it to Formula One. This experience has given me an intimate understanding of the desire required to make it at the top level of motorsports. I also have racing experience on both sides of the Atlantic Ocean and understand how the American definition of desire differs from the European understanding of that word.

After 20 years of racing and working in American motorsports, I have reason to question the desire of some young American race car drivers. America as a country has always provided a surplus of activities for teenagers, and in many cases, this seems to have created a comfort zone that leads young hopefuls to question whether the effort is really worth it or not.

Never forget: nobody owes you anything. Life in general owes you nothing. You get what you deserve, and you reach heights using steps on the ladder that you yourself create.

Consider this: Are you prepared to give up your comforts and social life to dedicate every waking hour to the betterment of your career? Are you prepared to work long hours with no thanks to help your career? Would you or your family be prepared to make alternate arrangements for your schooling if you had to spend extended time on the road? Would you or your family be prepared to forgo a college education to chase your dream of becoming a professional race car driver? These are all legitimate questions that you need to be able to answer.

In 1976, I lived in an old school bus and traveled from circuit to circuit in England while racing a Formula Ford. One day, while driving along England's main freeway, the M1, to a track in northern England, the diesel engine in the bus blew up. In one easy lesson, I learned all about grease, diesel, and dirt, as I rebuilt the engine, including having new valve seats fitted to the cylinder head and new crankshaft bearings. This was all done in a rest area while the English weather soaked and froze me.

Toward the end of the season in 1976, I had a throttle stick open, and the resulting high-speed crash destroyed my Formula Ford Hawke DL15 race car. I was so frightened by the impact that I collapsed when I was lifted from the car. My left leg was heavily bruised, had suffered permanent muscle damage, and was in a cast-like dressing for three weeks. Two days after the crash, and despite the considerable pain, I was in the factory cutting and welding my chassis because that was the only way I could get back on the track. I lived outside the factory in the car park . . . by myself. The days were long and sometimes lonely, but I never gave up.

At the racetracks each week, I would swap similar stories with other drivers from Brazil or France or wherever who were trying to achieve the same goals that I was. Despite our friendships, we would tear each other apart on the racetrack because winning was everything and giving up was just the easy way out.

British journalist Mark Hughes wrote the following about the great British former world champion, Nigel Mansell. Hughes was prompted to write this after again experiencing Mansell's desire and commitment at the Grand Prix Masters championship, when Mansell was the other side of the 50-year mark.

"A top F1 driver is a mass of competitive drives. Talent, while the number one prerequisite, is nowhere near enough on its own. To that basic baseline he needs to add supreme fitness and raw primeval desire or hunger. He has to want very badly to do it; the need to compete has to be hard-wired into him. The fitness levels won't normally interest him on an abstract level but are a means to an end, and as such, he's driven to achieve them. Not only will it help him physically in the car, but the spare mental capacity the fitness buys him will enable him to compete far more effectively.

"The desire factor is a fascinating one. The intensity of it is all that marks out a great driver from a good one. When Nigel Mansell was in a race car, he wrung the neck of his own abilities every time he sat in the car, driven to a degree that sometimes bordered on insanity. With a rival in his sights, you knew something was going to happen—either he'd pull off the big move, or there would be an incident. It sent a shiver down the spine. Who knows what drove him to such a place?"

Hughes remains convinced that a very big part of what made Mansell the driver he was, was showing the racing world just how wrong it had got him; proving the bastards wrong while at the same time lapping up the adulation of Mansellmania, taking great satisfaction from how people with no knowledge of the sport had seen what the racing world still struggled to see: that he was a very great driver.

That drive and desire were still evident as the Grand Prix Masters championship unfolded in 2005. Hughes also reasoned that it was difficult to see anyone else on the entry list of Grand Prix Masters that would be able to match Mansell's exceptional drive and desire. Has anyone ever said that about you, or will someone ever make that comment about you in the future?

I often wonder if the same desire is alive and well today? Has today's society changed the way we think about what type of effort should be expected to achieve anything significant?

AMERICAN MENTALITY

In 1984, Rick Mears and I were in Methodist Hospital in Indianapolis. Unfortunately, we were both recovering from devastating injuries from two Indy car crashes two weeks apart. We each had smashed feet and ankles and significant other orthopedic injuries that required multiple surgeries with bone and skin grafting. I had something like nine different surgeries, and Mears had even more. The therapy just to walk again was a minimum of two years.

After a two-month stay in the hospital, I was discharged to a rehabilitation center. Before I left, I wheeled myself into Mears' room and asked him if he thought he would ever race again. He paused, looked me in the eye, and told me that he would because the same desire to race he had prior to the devastating injuries was still burning within him. I told him I felt the same way, and we both went back to racing for most of the next decade.

Another great example of desire involves Scott Pruett. Pruett was king of karting when he moved into cars, and he really was considered by many, including some executives at Ford, to be the next American superstar. Ford was beginning to support Pruett's career, and there was even talk of a Formula One test with a Ford-powered car.

While he did all the normal things, such as meeting people and driving everything he could get his hands on, Pruett was not able to break into the big time without taking a huge personal financial risk. To prove to everybody that he had the talent he believed he had, Pruett sold his house, gathered up all his personal worth (which was $75,000), and gave it to Dick Simon for a seat at the Long Beach Grand Prix in 1988. During the race, the engine blew up, but not before he did enough to get noticed by team managers. Later that season, when Kevin Cogan broke his arm, the Machinists Union–sponsored team called upon Pruett to fill in, and his career path continued upward. Although a serious testing accident in 1990 almost ended Pruett's career, he came back to win Indy car races and make a very successful career for himself.

How many people do you know today who could display the same burning desire and commit all of their personal wealth to prove that they have the talent to succeed?

GOLDEN OPPORTUNITY SQUANDERED

During the Team Green Academy driver-development program in 1996 and 1997, we had several examples of what I call "pure desire" to succeed and then an unfortunate example of what I termed "dud desire."

One of the drivers to come through our program was Paul Edwards. He was very quick and very determined, but most of all, he had a great heart and passion for what he was doing and a great desire to succeed.

Edwards left his home comforts and enviable California lifestyle to live like a gypsy in England, knocking on all doors that might help him in his quest to become a professional race car driver. How many drivers do you know who would give up all the knowns about their lifestyles and plunge into the uncertainty of the unknowns in a country half a world away?

After years in Formula Fords, Edwards eventually made it to the British Formula Three championship. The British Formula Three championship has a habit of developing Formula One drivers, but alas Edwards' efforts collapsed halfway through the season because of a lack of adequate funding. At all times, though, Edwards showed the type of desire that Mario Andretti talked about, and that type of desire will eventually pay off, perhaps in some other endeavor.

By contrast, Team Green Academy winner Jeff Shafer was the epitome of a young driver who had everything he needed to be a champion *except* desire. I still believe today that Shafer was on his way to being a very successful professional race car driver with the world at his feet. It was not to be, however, because of that missing magic ingredient that Mario Andretti fully understands—desire. He was the epitome of a golden opportunity squandered.

While he was in the Team Green driver-development program, Shafer asked me many times to become his manager. While he was contracted to Team Green, I was not in a position to personally help because of a conflict of interest with the Derek Daly Performance Driving Academy.

At the end of 1997, Brown & Williamson pulled the plug on the driver-development program, and I decided to manage

Shafer's career. The first thing was to get him some stability, and I managed to negotiate a five-year contract with Forsythe Racing. Because he had not done many races the year before, it was decided to send him to Europe for the Palmer Audi series. He would get to race 19 times, he would have to adapt to a new culture, learn all new tracks, and race against the European road racing mentality.

To help keep his profile high in the United States while he raced in Europe, we arranged for Shafer to have his own driver's column in *On Track* magazine (America's motorsports magazine at the time). I then started discussions with Speedvision about televising the Palmer Audi series in the United States with a special American focus featuring Shafer at every race. To keep him happy while he played on the water at home in Las Vegas, Shafer also had a contract with Bombardier Sea Doo that supplied him with water toys. He was paid a significant salary, which I believe made him the highest-paid fringe professional in England that year.

After Shafer's first test sessions at Snetterton in England, he was within 1/10th of the fastest driver. Series owner Jonathan Palmer called me himself to state how impressive he thought Shafer was. Palmer said how good it might be for his series to have an American possibly win it.

While I was setting all of this up, I called two friends who were managing drivers. One was my former teammate at Williams in 1982, Formula One world champion Keke

Rosberg, who was managing Mika Hakkinen. The other was David Sears, who ran the most successful Formula 3000 race team in Europe and managed drivers like Sébastien Bourdais, Bruno Junqueira, and Juan Montoya. They helped me structure a fair contract that called for no payment from Shafer until he started earning enough to pay a management fee. The last thing I did was set up a company for him and secure a trusted money manager.

About three races into the season, I began to get alarmed by some of Shafer's actions, or should I say his lack of actions. I had arranged for him to drive the factory BMW M3 in the American Le Mans event at the Las Vegas Motor Speedway on one of his off weekends from England. I assumed that he would grab the opportunity with both hands, be present at all times, make himself useful whenever possible, and generally begin to show his desire. Instead of being in the pit lane during practice sessions, Shafer was on nearby Lake Mead fixing some boat engine. Now, he was a very laidback California boy who always walked to the beat of his own drum, and this was one of his endearing qualities, but a total disregard for getting to know the cars and people when they were under his nose alarmed me.

More alarm bells went off almost immediately. The living accommodations in England were not good enough for Shafer and his new wife. Living in England seemed to be hard for them. Instead of being a great adventure that would create the foundation on which his career would stand, it became a burden.

The coffin of his career was finally nailed shut when, instead of accepting my contract as his manager, Shafer presented me with the terms under which he would allow me to manage him. It was full of absurd clauses that were obviously written by an attorney ignorant of the sport and how it operated. Shafer seemed to be ill-advised and, sadly, the trust factor that we needed was obviously not there anymore.

We had many discussions across the ocean, and Jerry Forsythe spelled out the consequences of his actions. Shafer's decision was to get married, have a baby, and dedicate his life to something other than race car driving. I cancelled my management agreement with him. Forsythe Racing fulfilled its obligation until the end of the year and then terminated his contract.

I was personally bewildered by his actions, to the point that I asked myself the hard question: Do American drivers in general have the desire it takes to become successful as a race car driver? Jeff Shafer had desire, but it was not directed at becoming a professional race car driver. The answer to the general question, of course, was yes. Some American drivers do have the desire necessary.

A good example would be Jeff Gordon. When Gordon was 15 years old, he left his home in California and moved to Indiana. The only reason for the move was because there was more racing in Indiana. Gordon sought out supporters who would help him to display his talents. The first time I met him was in the pit lane at Indianapolis Raceway Park, where he was walking around a plain white Ford Thunderbird that belonged to a team that was about to let him drive its car. Even as a boyish teenager it was obvious that his focus was on doing everything within his power to drive race cars very fast.

How many teenagers do you currently know who would leave home and/or drive all over this country to race? Long days and nights of inconvenience on the road, sleeping in cars or trucks on nonstop trips that view the sunrise more than once on the same trip? How long will it last for some of them? When will some of them just tire of the grind? How many of these teenagers can separate the want to race from the need to race? "Want" and "need" separate the true desire from the pretender. Make no mistake about it, a career in motorsports will be tough, demanding, and more than most people can cope with. You will be beaten down, told no, rejected, and abused by your competitors and sometimes by your family. You will have bad days and then even worse days. You will ask yourself if it is all worth it. Your maturity level will be tested, and you will be forced to grow up rapidly.

Do you want to race for yourself or for someone else? Are you doing this for yourself or for your family? If it all stopped in the morning, would you miss it? Hidden behind all these questions is the answer to whether you have the desire or not to pursue the big time.

One of the easier ways to measure desire is in younger kids. Let's say a 10-year-old is chomping at the bit to go drive his kart. As soon as you get to the track and do a few runs, you then hear, "How long do we have to stay?" "Can we go home?"

That immediately shows that the desire to have fun with the activity outweighed the desire to do it for what I call "need reasons." This is understandable and acceptable for very young drivers, but I would become suspicious if that behavior continued into the mid-teen years. Remember, there is a huge difference between a want to do something and a need to do it.

Need is directly proportional to desire. The drivers who display what I call the "righteous desire" and true passion seem to attract others who recognize their focus and are willing to help the cause.

In 1990, I won the Sebring 12-hour race driving the dominant car of the time, the Nissan GTP ZX Turbo. It was a very satisfying win because I ended up driving almost 8 hours of the race. It had been close to 11 years since my last international win of significance. During those 11 years, I had pushed as hard as ever to get to the top of the rostrum. However, having reached the top, the feeling when I got there was just not what I had expected. The sense of satisfaction did not give me the buzz that I was expecting. I very quickly realized that for me, at that time of my life and career, the search for success behind the wheel of a race car no longer held the same significance.

That was the day that I knew my desire to dedicate my life to driving race cars was beginning to change. The will to push myself physically and mentally every day was no longer as strong as when I drove Formula One or Indy cars. I knew that the Sebring win was the beginning of the end of my driving career. Just over two years later, I walked away from the only life I had ever known.

If you are presented with opportunities, will you be prepared to make sacrifices? Are your comforts too comfortable? Can you get comfortable being uncomfortable? Would you leave the warm surroundings of your home and move to Japan like former Ferrari driver Eddie Irvine did to continue growing your career? Do you know what the difference is between making an emotional decision versus a heart-driven decision? The heart-driven decisions are the measure of a driver's desire. When desire is abundant, it's amazing the number of people who appear and want to help with the cause. Are you able to put yourself in that position? Desire cannot be created; you have it or you don't.

COMMITMENT

Commitment is also noncoachable. Just like desire, commitment is quantifiable but not through measurement by equipment. Without true commitment, it is doubtful that many successful drivers would have made it to the top. Commitment is doing whatever it takes to succeed. The most easily visible manifestation of commitment is a driver's work ethic, and it is really easy to recognize different work ethics among drivers.

True commitment is like a vow, and it will be seriously challenged many times along the journey. What sets apart those who stay true to their personal commitments is also what sets apart those who can persevere through the pain and frustrations of motor racing's very challenging obstacle course.

Stories abound about drivers who showed commitment. Many young karters will take jobs at kart shops just to be close to the sport they love. Would-be race car drivers will take summer jobs with racing schools to be close to race cars. They will build their own cars, live together in one-room apartments, and basically do anything to keep themselves in racing. If they have some money, they will automatically direct it toward something that will help their race programs. While their friends are out partying and traveling, the race car drivers will be somewhere else saving money.

One of the real challenges will come when the college education has to be put on hold because attending classes would take too much time out of the day. Try that one on with most parents and see what type of support you get. Jeff Gordon did this without hesitation, as did Fernando Alonso, Jimmy Johnson, and Rick Mears. It does not have to be this way, as American NASCAR driver Ryan Newman showed when he studied for his degree while he raced professionally. Finnish F1 driver Nico Rosberg also had a seat held for him at the Royal College of London University just in case his F1 dream did not happen.

When you are deciding whether or not it makes sense to delay getting a college education, let me offer this. I believe that all those with world-class talent get the opportunity to show their talents eventually. The key is knowing whether your driver has world-class talent or not. The difficult decision for parents comes when you do not really know whether your driver possesses that rare talent or not. Parents will usually make emotional decisions about their drivers (thinking that their offspring is as fast as anyone) rather than intellectual decisions, and that's what gets families into trouble.

There is no easy way to know how good your driver is. Drivers develop at different rates. Two drivers who are chasing the same dream can have very similar performance abilities at 15 years of age. The same two drivers one year later can have very different abilities because one driver can develop at a greater rate than the other. So what does a parent do when faced with the dilemma of career versus education? If you as a parent state that your driver must complete his college education before he concentrates on a motorsports career, then that could mean that the priorities are divided. Divided priorities could mean a lack of total commitment to the task of being a race car driver. One of the options to consider is that race car drivers can get their high school diplomas and college degrees online.

Grasping the potential of drivers is a specialized area only understood by experienced motorsports experts. This is why the education versus motorsports career decision for teenagers can be a gamble. The odds of making it as a professional race car driver are slim. As I stated before, however, I believe that a true world-class driving talent always gets the chance to show his talents.

Bold, defiant, and unflinching. This is a real glimpse into the mind of a committed champion.

Your desire to do something is complemented by your commitment to get it done. You might want to be a champion and might visualize yourself celebrating on the rostrum, but no matter what your desire is, it will go nowhere unless you have the commitment to do whatever it takes to make it happen.

You have heard that when the going gets tough, the tough get going. It has never been so true as it is for race car drivers. Shortly after he announced his retirement, Michael Schumacher responded to criticism of his often-controversial driving style in England's *Autosport* magazine. He said he could not argue with observers and fellow drivers who labeled him selfish over 15 years in Formula One. "I agree with that," he said. "Why should I give anything to anyone when we're on the track?"

Schumacher's career was punctuated by moments of highly aggressive driving, including the clash with Damon Hill at the 1994 Australian Grand Prix that decided the world championship in his favor. He also hit Jacques Villeneuve at the 1997 European Grand Prix, taking himself out of the race and allowing Villeneuve to become the world champion. Perhaps one of his most controversial moments might have been his bungled attempt to disrupt the last moments of qualifying in Monaco in 2006, when Alonso was slowed while attempting to take pole position.

To these accusations, Schumacher simply suggested that his detractors were just misguided. "To be honest, if the other drivers criticize me, then it means I've done things the right way," he said.

Motor racing will test your resolve unlike any other sport. Your success is not usually determined by your level of raw talent. There are many variables that depend on the strengths of many others, and you must rely on before you can display your talents. Seldom do all these forces work in harmony when a driver is in his formative years. Frustration can be considered a filter that separates whole-hearted from half-hearted commitment. Always remember that the only place where success comes before work is in the dictionary.

Could a cultural background somehow breed the desire to succeed in one nation more so than in another? Do the comforts of America, for example, contribute to the failure of America's drivers on the world stage? Some people think the answer to this question is yes. Michael Andretti's attempt to become established in Formula One is a great example of what the McLaren Formula One team deemed to be a weak commitment. Andretti had proven to the world that he was very gifted and had risen to the top of open-wheel racing in America. He signed with the McLaren Formula One team as teammate to the great Ayrton Senna. I traveled the world that year, covering Andretti's every move for ESPN sports television. One of the reasons I became intrigued by his failure was that I believed, and still do, that he was one of the most talented drivers in the world. What was missing? The McLaren team thought it was commitment.

I traveled to many of Andretti's Formula One races, and each Friday I would take up a variety of vantage points out on the circuits. As I watched him during practice and qualifying sessions, I saw a driver who did not drive with the style I knew he possessed. He looked awkward and did not seem to fit the car or team. His timing was off, and the fluid, confident style that Andretti had developed was somehow suppressed.

Andretti was criticized in Europe for not participating in the Formula One lifestyle by deciding not to move to Europe but to live in Nazareth, Pennsylvania. He would use the family plane to get him to the New York airport, where he would board a Concord for the transatlantic flight. The comforts of home were deemed to be more important to him than being closer to the team in England.

This was a challenging time for McLaren, as it had lost its manufacturer engine deal and had replaced it with a Ford Cosworth engine. It was also a time when the rules of Formula One changed to allow only 12 laps of practice per session. These two moves stacked the odds against Andretti, but teammate Ayrton Senna proved that they were not insurmountable changes. Senna also seemed to recognize Andretti's talent and was a supporter of his teammate.

The season did not start off well for Andretti, with an engine stall on the grid in South Africa. It went from bad to worse, with many first-lap crashes. At a time when the team was frustrated with Andretti's performance, there was a feeling within the team that instead of working through the issues with the team, Andretti retreated to the comforts of home in Pennsylvania. The team viewed this as a lack of commitment from Andretti.

The commitment you make to a team will be reflected in the commitment they make to you. It is my belief that by not making the lifestyle commitment to live in Europe, Andretti sent a message to the team that he was not prepared to make the necessary sacrifices. I believe his lack of a *total* commitment was felt by McLaren, and I believe that their commitment to him was in turn weak, and the spiral started to go downhill from there.

Many years later, American journalist Matt Davis wrote an interesting story that described Andretti's plight and posed some questions that highlighted the cultural backgrounds.

"The last American F1 driver was Michael Andretti in 1993—a terrible season with McLaren-Ford in which Andretti showed absolutely no sign of wanting to commit to the rarefied atmosphere of international Formula car racing. He'd fly in for each race and fly back to Pennsylvania immediately afterward, making almost no effort to ingratiate himself with his fellow crewmembers. Which was fine by one Mika Hakkinen, who jumped into Andretti's seat before it even had a chance to cool, going on to do pretty well, I'd say. [Mika Hakkinen went on to become a two-time world champion.]

"So what's preventing America and American drivers from getting into the Formula One scene?

"Talking with broadcast legend Chris Economaki, and some European journalists, here's some of what came up in Davis' conversations:

"American drivers aren't hungry enough. In fact, they're lazy by European standards.

"American drivers expect to make money almost immediately, whereas drivers on the international circuit invest for years out of love for the sport and feel blessed if they break even.

"American drivers do not live and work outside of America easily, struggling to accept the cultural and attitudinal differences that are the reality of being away from home.

"American drivers are great once the tires are hot and grippy but are terrible during qualifying runs on fresh slicks.

"American drivers in series outside the United States almost always blame the equipment, crew, and/or other drivers for everything that goes wrong instead of diving in, pinpointing the real source of the problem, and addressing it.

"Not all of these are unique to us, certainly, but where does this leave us? Not an easy one to answer. Are we incurable homebodies incapable of leaving the nest and taking on multiple struggles behind the wheel in foreign lands? Ugly Americans? Some would say yes."

I believe this type of story, although relevant in some areas, misses the point. Andretti failed because his commitment level did not nearly match his talent level. He was also going through a difficult personal crisis at that time with his wife, Sandra. More than likely his decision-making was influenced by his problems at home (perhaps a challenge to his mental skills).

I became aware of Andretti's problems at the Italian Grand Prix that year, and I immediately called his manager, John Caponigro, in Detroit. I suggested that unless Andretti got rid of his emotional baggage quickly, he would not make it in Formula One. I had a solid personal relationship with Caponigro and therefore did not fear making such a bold statement. I saw it as a crisis, and I discussed it as a supporter and admirer of Andretti's, yet Caponigro was not in a position to create such an upheaval in Andretti's life. The personal issues eventually resulted in divorce.

For whatever reason, the above included, Andretti's quest failed. Even though it might have been difficult, the cold hard facts are that he didn't do whatever it would take. One of the world's most talented drivers did not quite have all the pieces of the Champion's Pyramid needed to succeed in the Formula One environment.

Michael Schumacher was the complete opposite. He oozed commitment. Commitment was a way of life for Schumacher. Commitment was a habit for him. *Autosport*'s Nigel Roebuck once wrote, "Michael earns the respect of all the people around him: people know he's committed and doing the best job he can, so naturally everyone around him does the same—you don't have to motivate people very much when Michael's around."

Danica Patrick is a good example of a driver who beat the odds. In such a male-dominated sport, she stood her ground, eventually got the right break, and made it into the big time. In *Autosport* magazine, Patrick relates her feeling that her strengths are definitely "determination to make it and perseverance."

Formula One is regarded as the pinnacle of motorsports in the world, and some drivers from this arena are exceptionally dedicated. Alain Prost worked hard at his craft, Ayrton Senna poured over data for hours on race weekends, and Michael Schumacher is considered the hardest worker of them all.

When Schumacher retired from Ferrari, everybody considered Kimi Raikkonen to be arguably the fastest man in Formula One and therefore a worthy replacement to Schumacher. It was interesting to read the comments about Raikkonen from the professionals who either worked with or alongside Schumacher.

Ferrari's technical director Ross Brawn said, "[Raikkonen] has incredible speed, but none of us have experienced working with him yet, so that will be a new aspect for us."

Former Jordan F1 designer Gary Anderson was even concerned about how Schumacher's departure would impact his teammate. "Kimi has a different work ethic from Michael, and it will be interesting to see how Felipe Massa responds to that," Anderson said. "With Michael there, you had the impression that he worked hard because Michael was the benchmark. Without Michael, that will change."

After Michael retired, a journalist I respect greatly, Jonathan Noble, wrote a very interesting story in *Racer* magazine. He cited an unnamed Formula One team manager as saying, "Kimi is absolutely magical. He is the kind of talent that you see only once in 10 or 15 years."

The manager then wondered how he had missed Raikkonen as he rose through the lower formulae. He said that "Kimi had amazing speed . . . he lived to drive Formula One cars on the absolute limit." What he said next caught my attention. He said, "Kimi would never become a champion at Ferrari unless he changed the brain in his head. He was nowhere near Michael when it comes to commitment application to the job and just working hard. It's sad but its true."

How many drivers do you know with the same type of commitment as Michael Schumacher? Do you personally have the type of commitment needed to make it to the very top? Will your personal commitment level help or hinder your career? Is there any truth in the above story?

Commitment is something you can work on. Put simply, your actions will be the measure of your commitment. When you make sacrifices to achieve a goal, you demonstrate commitment to that goal.

If you consistently find yourself making compromises with your life in order to keep racing—whether that means staying home and getting a good night's sleep the night before a race rather than going out with your friends, or working all summer at a race shop in order to make enough money to help pay for your racing—those actions indicate your commitment.

If you really want to succeed, you will need to evaluate the decisions you make with regard to your racing.

DRIVERS WITH THE CHAMPION'S PYRAMID

The Champion's Pyramid is a bit like a house. It might look similar to the one beside it, but everything is in fact just a little different. Every champion has a different version of the Champion's Pyramid. In years past, a Champion's Pyramid looked different because the necessary physical preparedness was nowhere near the level it has become in this day and age. Just like all other sports played out on a world stage, every year that passes makes the sport more and more specialized. In years to come, we will probably marvel at the lengths champions go in order to be the best they can be. Michael Schumacher's blood sampling during test sessions to accurately evaluate his fitness levels—although leading edge at the time—might seem archaic in the years to come.

If you suspect I am a big fan of Senna and Schumacher, you are correct. In my opinion, Schumacher is the most complete driver ever. Others who built a complete pyramid of skills include: Fernando Alonso, Mario Andretti, Sébastien Bourdais, Gil de Ferran, Dale Earnhardt Sr., Jeff Gordon, Alain Prost, Ayrton Senna, and Jackie Stewart.

Remember, as I mentioned earlier, you do not have to have the Champion's Pyramid fully developed to win races at the highest levels. Both Juan Montoya and Kimi Raikkonen have proven that. Consider what three-time world champion Jackie Stewart said about Kimi and his future potential in May 2007 to the British newspaper, *The Telegraph*: "The way he lives his life is contrary to the complete package, the kind that allowed Schumacher to win multiple championships, (as well as) Senna and Prost, Jim Clark, or even me."

In the *Daily Express*, Stewart reportedly added: "It is an attitude, a mentality, a way of doing business. Our lifestyle, mind, make-up was different from a Raikkonen—or for that matter a Jenson Button.

"There are other things in Raikkonen's life he still wishes to carry on doing," Stewart continued. "He doesn't seem prepared to make the sacrifice of reducing the lifestyle he has chosen because he enjoys it. He is not prepared to compromise."

In the *Times*, Stewart accused Ferrari's Raikkonen of being "oblivious of social skills," and a cursory search for his name at youtube.com shows the Finn falling off a yacht, apparently drunk.

Let me ask you one question: Does Raikkonen strike you as a driver who is committed to building the Champion's Pyramid as I have laid out here? Will Raikkonen have sustained greatness against the best competition in the world? If you got to Formula One, what decisions would you make? What would you commit to doing in an effort to be the very best you can be? These are all questions that can and will be answered by all champions in the future.

Although the 2005/2006 Formula One world champion, Fernando Alonso, is showing that he has what we are calling the Champion's Pyramid, we do not yet know if he has the desire and commitment that Michael Schumacher has shown; only time will tell us that.

To give you insight into Alonso, let's look at some comments made by the men closest to him on the championship-winning

Renault team. These comments were made after Alonso won the first of his world championships.

First, Executive Director of Engineering Pat Symonds had this to say: "I think the main thing Fernando has, and which every champion needs, is intelligence. I won't say he won his championship by driving tactically, but he assured himself of the championship by driving tactically. What he did was very carefully control himself and do what he needed to do to get the championship. And that shows a lot of maturity and restraint.

"There were times when I'd argue that his restraint was almost a little too much, and I felt that we could race a little bit harder. But, he does have this very deep understanding of how to go racing. He is remarkably good at understanding what's going on in the race, what needs to be done, reading the race, and exploiting it well. It really is one of his strengths, and it's a strength he shares with the other two champions I've worked with: Ayrton Senna and Michael Schumacher. If a guy drives a car and comes into the pits and doesn't know why he's gone quick or what the hell's going on, he's really at a disadvantage. There are some like that, but Fernando is not like that at all.

"A trait of great drivers is to adapt. A driver needs to work hard on the setups of his car for as long as he can, but there comes a time on Sunday when that's it, that's what you've got . . . and that might even change if it rains.

"His technical understanding is good enough. I don't want engineers driving the car. I want people who can report honestly and accurately what's going on, and if they can't say, they can't. One of the things I like about Fernando is that if you make a change on the car and he can't feel it, he says it feels the same. He doesn't give you a long spiel. His race craft improves all the time, his maturity comes on. I don't think he can drive any faster now than when he started; I think that is sort of fixed. I think it's the understanding that improves. And he does work very hard at it now.

"If you ask where can he improve, I couldn't tell you. What I suspect is that he is 95, 97, or 99 percent. He certainly doesn't have any weaknesses that he needs to address.

"The pressure of leading the championship did not seem to affect him. For someone his age, and doing it for the first time, the coolness was stunning."

His race engineer, Remi Tallin, painted this picture of the champion: "I would think that the best point for him is that he's always ready to listen. He's quite happy to tackle technical things, and that's something we do quite often. On top of that, he wanted to know what he's going to be driving. He wants to know every part of the car or the engine or the gearbox. So basically in a race and even without our advice, he can deal with something in the car that can help us.

"He's like a leader in the team, and he's involved with everybody—the mechanics, engine technicians, marketing, whatever. He tries to make everybody go in the same direction, and I think that's the best thing about him. Four years ago, he was a small child in the back of the garage. Now he's like a man in the front of the garage, pulling everybody together."

Alonso's chief mechanic, Chris Hessey, said this: "He always recognizes the job the guys have done on the car for him. After the race, he always comes and speaks to us and says, 'Thank you, the car was perfect.' One night in Brazil, I went up to him and said, 'What's it like to be world champion?' He said, 'What's it like for you to be world champion?' Without the crew, he could not have accomplished the feat and he wanted to recognize us for that."

The above statements by the men closest to him show that Alonso has a mix of feel talent (he can engineer the car) and instinct-reflex talent (he can drive it really fast). He can also communicate well and has great mental skills. He is obviously fit enough to drive Formula One cars for the course of a race distance, and most of all he displays the desire and commitment to chase his dream and be the very best he can be. He has the Champion's Pyramid fully developed.

THE VERY BEST

Although there are many great examples of drivers who have fully developed the Champion's Pyramid, few would disagree that if you were to model yourself and understand what it really takes to become truly successful, you should look hard at the career of Michael Schumacher. The technical directors of his two championship-winning teams, Ross Brawn from Ferrari and Pat Symonds from Renault, were united in their assessment of Schumacher, saying that he motivates and inspires people within the teams. He brings everybody together unlike anybody in the sport before him.

His on-track performance was what inspired his teams more than anything else. In motorsports, team members will work day and night for a driver who gives every ounce when he is in the race car. From day one in a Formula One car to the last day of his career, Schumacher drove every lap and every corner like a qualifying lap. Sixteen years later he was still driving every lap the same way, setting the fastest race lap in his last race, the Brazilian Grand Prix. That commitment to bring your "A" game every day is part of what inspires teams to be the very best.

After Schumacher's final Grand Prix, Speed TV announcer Bob Varsha probably put it best when he said: "Michael was a selfish opportunist who never criticized his team, and a driver who reset the standards by which those who will follow will be judged. That ruthless driver obliterated every race record of note with 68 poles and 91 victories in 16 glorious seasons."

There is no doubt that Michael Schumacher had the most fully developed Champion's Pyramid ever.

How many drivers have ever separated themselves from the rest with this type of quality, and how many drivers in the future will do so? Are you a driver with these qualities? Would you like to have these qualities? What would you personally do to develop all of the qualities of the Champion's Pyramid? Only you can answer those questions, and your answers will determine how high you fly.

EPILOGUE

It is a well-known fact that you are more than halfway to solving a problem when you identify it. Becoming a motorsports champion involves many problems, and I hope I have given you some of the answers to the issues that most drivers face. Large team budgets are sometimes wasted because the foundation is not solid and the execution of the job at hand is not carried out efficiently or effectively. Ex-karter Michael Schumacher has proven that the most successful teams are led by the driver.

Within the pages of this book, I have given you a key to a big door. The next step is for you to walk through the door yourself. However, to get through the door, you have to cross terrain that requires specific skills and dedication. If you were not blessed with all the supplemental skills required to be a champion naturally, it is my belief that you can acquire them. I believe world champions Damon Hill, Graham Hill, and Nigel Mansell would agree. So also would Indy 500 champions Eddie Cheever, Gordon Johncock, Buddy Lazier, and Johnny Rutherford. These are all drivers who worked at developing the skills necessary to be successful.

What you learn on the racetrack is the tangible part. What you learn away from the track is the intangible. The intangible can also be the difference between the amount of hardware you will actually have in your trophy cabinet and the amount you might have had.

The autobiographies of great champions are littered with stories of struggle, pain, and sometimes despair. In an era when motorsports has become so specialized, becoming a professional race car driver while attending high school or college is nearly impossible. Successful motorsports is not just a passion, it's a lifestyle. It is a dedication of one's life to the requirements of the career. It is a selfish pursuit where relationships sometimes suffer, and understanding partners are almost impossible to find. It is a colorful, glamorous, savage sport of gladiators who sometimes pay the ultimate price with their lives. It is an emotionally charged atmosphere, where the chase has sometimes left the pursuers both emotionally and financially bankrupt.

It is also one of the world's most satisfying endeavors. The physical difficulties and sacrifices are dwarfed by the golden satisfaction of competition and success. When a driver's talent is exposed, the decision-making is tested to the fullest, and the adrenaline fills the veins through a pounding heart, being first to the finish is everything.

The road has now been laid out for you. Now it's up to you to start making your way down that road. Are you ready to make these choices? If you say yes, your life will change. How you live your life will change. How you view yourself and how others view you will change. You will think and act differently. My challenge to you is this: in your private, quiet time, are you ready to make the choices that can build your own Champion's Pyramid? If the answer is yes, then follow these guidelines.

Focus on being a champion rather than on becoming one. Fill your mind with good, wholesome thoughts. You have 100 percent control over what you think, and what you think can be the greatest power you possess.

Strive to be a champion in the way you lead your life, not just in how you approach your racing. This will ultimately demand a mature, solid, and confident mindset that keeps things in perspective. Remember what confidence is about because it shouldn't be about an outcome. Rather, it should be about a strong inner belief—in fact, an unshakable knowledge—that no matter how big the challenge, no matter how tough the going gets, you can count on yourself to bring the best you've got to every performance. To consistently deliver maximum effort each time, win, lose, or draw. Even if things don't go well on a given weekend as far as the final results are concerned, you can still be 100 percent successful if your personal yardstick is calibrated this way. It's up to you; it's your choice, and choice can be the greatest power you have.

Focus on the process of personal excellence, being in the moment, and bringing the best you've got to everything that you do. Enjoy the process—take the time on a regular basis to stop and sniff the flowers along the way—and be satisfied that whatever the result is, you've done your part to the fullest. That is the hallmark of the true champion.

I have really enjoyed putting my thoughts down on paper, and I hope you have found the stories and analogies both interesting and informative. I learned a lot about what I have written by recognizing my own weaknesses and consequently looking deeper into the makeup of the great champions. My hope, and indeed my whole reason for writing this book, is to make you think a little more. To make you a little more aware of what might be just around the corner, and to give you the ability to take a step that you might not have been able to take by yourself. However, always remember that we are all individuals with unique qualities. Use the information given to supplement and stretch your own person. Do *not* use the information to try to become someone you are not. Stay true to yourself, and enjoy the success. There will be joy in the journey, and I will enjoy seeing some of you on the rostrum.

Best wishes,

Derek Daly

DRIVER'S RESOURCES

PITFIT TRAINING

PitFit Training is the recognized leader in developing driver-specific fitness, nutrition, and human-performance programs to expressly address the physical and mental demands of the motorsports industry. PitFit was founded in 1997 by Jim Leo. Leo and the PitFit crew provide fitness training to racers in various series, including the IRL, Champ Car world series, Formula BMW, Toyota Atlantics, Indy Pro series, USAC, karting, and more. To schedule an interview, contact Jim Leo at 317-388-1000 or jleo@pitfit.com. To learn more, visit www.pitfit.com.

ST. VINCENT SPORTS MEDICINE ADMINISTRATIVE OFFICE

8227 Northwest Boulevard, Suite 160

Indianapolis, IN 46278

Phone: 317-415-5747

Toll Free: 800-277-8817

Fax: 317-415-5748

St.Vincent Sports Medicine is the largest hospital-based sports medicine program in the state of Indiana. Drivers and teams, such as Scott Dixon, Dario Franchitti, Dan Wheldon, and the Panther Indy Car team, use St. Vincent for their physical conditioning requirements.

HUMAN PERFORMANCE INTERNATIONAL

There are many sports psychologists who work with athletes; however, I believe you need to choose someone who has a firm understanding of the requirements of motorsports. Dr. Jacques Dallaire of Human Performance International (HPI, www.human-performance.com) is one of those people. He has dedicated a large portion of his life to developing race car drivers. I was one of his early studies when the late Dr. Dan Marisi was an active partner.

Human Performance International uses the principles of sport science technology to improve individual and group performance. The instructors individually coach participants on all aspects of physical and mental behavior for athletes at all levels and in all sports, the medical and rehabilitation community, the education community, the occupational and business community, older adults, and children.

In 1983, two scientists from Canada embarked on a mission to improve the performance of motorsports athletes and other high performers. They have had access to some of the world's greatest drivers, including Ayrton Senna and Nigel Mansell. To date, they have had hundreds of drivers come through their program, and their experiences are used to give mean average results to all drivers against the 20-plus years of their data bank.

As the programs have evolved, so have the number and variety of professionals who have sought out the assistance of HPI specialists to improve their performance. To date, HPI has worked with clients in virtually every form of motorsports, a broad selection of players from individual and team sports, law enforcement officers, surgeons, pilots, firefighters, sales professionals, corporate executives, and most recently, air traffic controllers. The mental skills in particular that underlie championship performance are common to all of these endeavors, which accounts for the diversity of the HPI clientele.

In the past, the majority of athletes have focused time and energy only on the development or training of the physical self, with little attention placed on the development of basic mental skills. That's because tools have not been available to effectively teach athletes how to focus and concentrate. HPI has produced a tool they call the Mindshaper training program, which teaches you how to focus and develop the right mental skills.

Several professional drivers use this product. The list includes NASCAR driver Ward Burton, Patrick Carpentier, two-time Indy 500 winner Helio Castroneves, and Ron Fellows.

GLORIA BUDD, MASTER PRACTITIONER OF NLP AND PERSONAL COACH

Another option for drivers looking for a personal coach is sports psychologist Gloria Budd from England (www.psyched-to-win.com). Budd has worked with many different athletes (including race car drivers) in a variety of sports and very much believes in personal coaching. When working with her athletes, she gets right to the heart of the matter with simple word pictures and visualization exercises. Budd helps drivers see what they want. After all, we are what we eat, and we are what we think.

She is a dynamic and inspirational coach who believes passionately in her work. She has certainly made her mark in the world of sports, and her successes with tennis players and racing drivers are already well documented in the national and international press.

Gloria writes: "Can you remember a moment in your life when you just knew that you were performing at your best, everything looked fantastic, you were 'buzzing' along and feeling great. What would it be like if you could do that again whenever you want to; in fact, why not right now?"

DRIVING SCHOOLS

Racing schools are a very good resource for parents and others as part of the development of a driver. My son, Conor, attended the Bertil Roos Racing School in Florida for his first taste of open-wheel cars and then progressed to the Skip Barber Racing School. I would highly recommend the Skip Barber Racing School because it has a nationwide racing series and very good coaches. Here is a list of some good race schools:

Bertil Roos Racing School
P.O. Box 221, Route 115
Blakeslee, PA 18610
1-800-722-3669
roos@epix.net

Bondurant Racing School
20000 S. Maricopa Rd. Gate 3
Chandler, AZ 85226
1-800-842-RACE

Bridgestone Racing Academy
Box 373
Pontypool, Ontario L0A 1K0
Canada
905-983-1114
http://www.race2000.com/

Jim Russell Racing Schools
Infineon Raceway
29355 Arnold Dr.
Sonoma, CA 95476
1-800-733-0345
sales@jimrussellusa.com

Skip Barber Racing School LLC
P.O. Box 1629
Lakeville, CT 06039
1-800-221-1131
speed@skipbarber.com

INDEX